CANADA

VERMONT

NEW HAMPSHIRE

MASSACHUSETTS

RHODE ISLAND

CONNECTICUT

NEW JERSEY

DELAWARE

MARYLAND

NEW YORK

● New York

PENNSYLVANIA

Philadelphia ●

GETTYSBURG ★

★ ANTIETAM

HARPERS FERRY ★

● Washington, D.C.

MANASSAS/BULL RUN ★

★ BRANDY STATION

★ CHANCELLORSVILLE

RICHMOND ●

■ FORT MONROE

APPOMATTOX ★

★ PETERSBURG/ FIVE FORKS

WEST VIRGINIA

VIRGINIA

LEXINGTON ●

★ PERRYVILLE

KENTUCKY

● RALEIGH

NORTH CAROLINA

NASHVILLE ★

★ MURFREESBORO

FRANKLIN ★

TENNESSEE

CHATTANOOGA

SHILOH ★

★ CHICKAMAUGA

PHIS

SOUTH CAROLINA

● Columbia

ATLANTA ★

★ AUGUSTA

★ CHARLESTON/ FORT SUMTER

ALABAMA

● MACON

GEORGIA

MONTGOMERY ●

● ANDERSONVILLE

★ SAVANNAH

MISSISSIPPI

MOBILE ★

APPALACHIAN MOUNTAINS

FLORIDA

New Orleans

GULF OF MEXICO

LAKE SUPERIOR

LAKE MICHIGAN

LAKE HURON

LAKE ERIE

LAKE ONTARIO

MICHIGAN

INDIANA

OHIO

ATLANTIC OCEAN

Legend:

UNITED STATES

CONFEDERATE STATES

TERRITORIES

CLAIMED BY BOTH SIDES

● CITIES

★ BATTLES

■ FORTS

AUG - - 2001

DORLING KINDERSLEY 📖 EYEWITNESS BOOKS

CIVIL WAR

2nd Battalion flag,
Hilliard's Alabama
Legion

Telescope

Canister
with lead slugs

Canteen and haversack

Ketchum hand grenade

Union private

DORLING KINDERSLEY ⅅⓀ EYEWITNESS BOOKS

CIVIL WAR

Written by
JOHN STANCHAK

Model 1850 saber

Confederate currency

The Great Seal of
the Confederacy

Infantry drum

.44 caliber Colt revolver

.58 caliber rifle

A Dorling Kindersley Book

DORLING **DK** KINDERSLEY

LONDON, NEW YORK, AUCKLAND, DELHI, JOHANNESBURG,
MUNICH, PARIS, and SYDNEY

Publisher Neal Porter
Executive Editor Iris Rosoff
Art Director Dirk Kaufman

Project Editor Andrea Curley
Designer Tom Carling, Carling Design, Inc.

Published in the United States by
Dorling Kindersley Publishing, Inc.
95 Madison Ave.
New York, New York 10016

First American Edition
2 4 6 8 10 9 7 5 3 1

Copyright © 2000
Dorling Kindersley Publishing, Inc.
Text copyright © 2000 by John Stanchak

Confederate soldier

Dorling Kindersley books are available at special discounts for bulk
purchases for sales promotions or premiums. Special editions, including
personalized covers, excerpts of existing guides, and corporate imprints
can be created in large quantities for specific needs. For more information,
contact Special Markets Dept., Dorling Kindersley Publishing, Inc.,
95 Madison Ave., New York, NY 10016; Fax: (800) 600-9098.

Library of Congress Cataloging-in-Publication Data

Stanchak, John E.
  Civil War / by John Stanchak — 1st American ed.
    p. cm. — (Dorling Kindersley eyewitness)
  Summary: Examines many aspects of the Civil War,
including the issue of slavery, secession, the raising of armies,
individual battles, the commanders, Northern life, Confederate
culture, the surrender of the South, and the aftermath.
  ISBN 0-7894-6302-4 (hc) ISBN 0-7894-6303-2 (pb)
  ISBN 0-7894-6988-X (lib.)
    1. United States — History — Civil War, 1861-1865 —
Juvenile literature [1. United States — History — Civil War,
1861-1865.] I. Title. II. Series

E468 .S795 2000   00-020431
973.7—dc21

Printed in China by Toppan Printing Co. (Shenzhen) Ltd.
Color reproduction by Colourscan, Singapore

Canvas-covered canteen

Confederate
General
Stand Watie

4th Regiment flag, Irish Brigade

Clara Barton

see our complete
catalog at
www.dk.com

Jacket of
Rush's Lancers

Slave auction poster

Contents

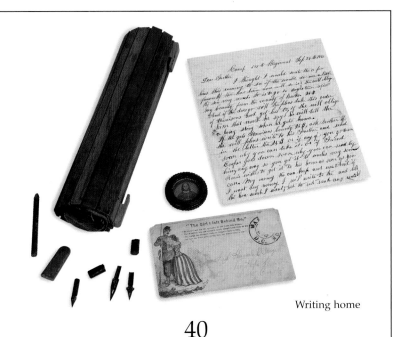

Writing home

The long argument

WHAT RIGHTS DOES A STATE ENJOY? Can it ignore a federal law with which it does not agree? Americans had been arguing about the powers of the national government versus the rights of states longer than they had been arguing about slavery. The issue of states' rights had caused shouting matches when America's founders were writing the U.S. Constitution in the late 1700s. During the 1830s, President Andrew Jackson had argued with South Carolina's legislators over a tariff law they did not want to enforce. Years later, the bickering revolved around the legality of slavery in new Western territories. If slaves were property and the right to own property was protected by the Constitution, could slave owners take their human property into territories or states where slavery was prohibited? In the 1850s, the argument erupted into guerrilla warfare between settlers in pro-slavery Missouri and their antislavery next-door neighbors in Kansas. Missouri Border Ruffians rode across the state line to burn farms and murder antislavery men. Kansas guerrillas, called Jayhawkers, retaliated. In time, the U.S. Army was called out to curtail this bloodletting. Some slave state patriots believed Southerners could never make peace with a strong national government. They called for states to leave the Union, a process called secession. In the prewar years, these secession advocates were called fire-eaters.

AN ANTISLAVERY SLOGAN
Americans who hated slavery formed organizations to try to end it and to embarrass slave owners. One group's slogan was the question "Am I Not a Man and a Brother?" The members tried to force masters to admit that slaves were not farm property, but people like themselves.

More captives on the afterdeck

Emaciated captives

SAVED FROM SLAVERY
The federal government outlawed the importation of new slaves from Africa in 1807. The South's need for more laborers was so great, however, that ship captains continued smuggling slaves into the country until the start of the Civil War. The people in this newspaper illustration were kidnapped in Africa in 1860. They were being shipped to the United States to be sold into slavery when U.S. Navy sailors rescued them.

A SECESSION PROPHET
Virginia agriculturist Edmund Ruffin believed the South had a different culture from the rest of the country. The publisher of a farming journal, he turned to writing articles that promoted the establishment of a separate Southern nation. In the 1850s, he became a leading fire-eater, and in 1860 helped South Carolinians organize their secession campaign. He was given the honor of firing the cannon shot at Fort Sumter, South Carolina, that began the Civil War. After the conflict, he committed suicide rather than live under Union rule.

THE CAPITAL OF A CRUMBLING NATION
While congressmen feuded over states' rights issues, two present-day symbols of Washington, D.C., were unfinished. In the months before the war, both the Capitol's dome and the Washington Monument were under construction. The capital was not a very impressive place to work out the nation's problems.

SOUTHERN CHIVALRY — ARGUMENT versus CLUB'S.

A VERY PUBLIC WHIPPING

Charles Sumner was a Massachusetts attorney who won national notice in the 1840s for representing an African American in what may have been the nation's first school desegregation case. Though he lost the case, he won the respect of state voters and was elected to the U.S. Senate in 1851. In 1856, Sumner stood on the floor of the Senate for two days speaking out against slavery and its supporters. Among the people he tongue-lashed was Andrew Butler, a senator from South Carolina. Butler was not present to reply. However, two days later, his nephew, South Carolina Congressman Preston Brooks, strode into the Senate and beat Sumner senseless with a cane. South Carolinians applauded Brooks for defending his family's honor.

Cassy ministering to Uncle Tom after his whipping

ANTISLAVERY MEN OF KANSAS

Armed with a cannon, these Kansas citizens are ready to fight pro-slavery raiders from Missouri. This photograph was taken in the 1850s, a decade that saw violence over the slavery issue grow all around the nation. A pro-slavery mob lynched the publisher of an antislavery newspaper in Alton, Illinois. A few Southern law officers were beaten when they tried to apprehend runaway slaves living in Northern towns.

THE BOOK THAT FUELED THE FLAMES

The novel *Uncle Tom's Cabin; or, Life among the Lowly* was published in 1852. It portrayed some cruelties of slavery, featured a wicked slave manager named Simon Legree, and excited readers with scenes of a chase after a runaway slave. This illustration from the book features its main character, a kind but abused slave named Uncle Tom. The book became wildly popular in the North and was turned into an even more popular play. Actors hated to perform it in pro-slavery towns, though, because performances caused fights and disorder.

Slave life

By the year 1860, most white Americans were embarrassed by slavery. After the American Revolution and its promise that "all men are created equal," the states north of Maryland abolished slavery. But in the South, plantation owners depended on slaves. Growing cotton, sugar, rice, and other crops in the hot weather required the labor of many people, and relatively few whites lived there. The region's richest planters believed that without slaves their economy would be ruined. Because they could not explain how people could be slaves in a nation where all were supposed to be free, they simply called this bondage the Peculiar Institution. Northerners continued to chide Southerners, and this made them angry. Many of them felt trapped by slavery too. Their representatives in the U.S. Congress told the rest of the nation to accept the situation. While white men argued, black slaves suffered. They were paid nothing, fed little, given poor clothing, and denied an education. Their masters could beat them at any time, and they and their families could be sold. Long before the Civil War, slavery was a moral and political problem that would not go away.

Slaves who grew tired of hearing the copper bells muffled the clappers with dirt and mud.

A SLAVE COLLAR
A slave could be worth several hundred dollars. If he or she escaped, it was a financial loss for the owner. If the master believed a slave was likely to run away, he sometimes kept track of the slave by locking him or her into this collar equipped with bells. As long as the master could hear the jingling of the bells, he knew his slave was close by.

Leg iron, which prevented a slave from bending the leg

Shackle

TOOLS OF CRUELTY
This photograph was circulated throughout the North by antislavery activists. The man in it is a former slave who posed in shackles and an iron slave collar for a Union army officer during the Civil War. A paddle used for beating slaves lay on the ground behind him.

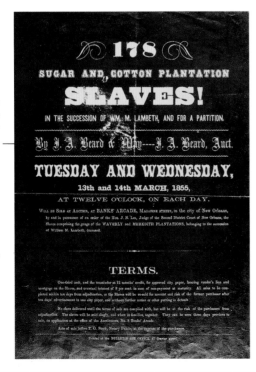

Auctioning slaves was a specialty for some of the auctioneering professionals.

ADVERTISING A SLAVE AUCTION
Slaves were sold at auctions. Before one of them was held, advertisements such as this one were circulated. They described the men and women who were being put up for sale.

AT WORK IN THE FIELDS
These cotton field hands labor under the supervision of a mounted overseer, a white manager of slaves who was employed by the owner of the plantation. Overseers were also expected to control and discipline slaves. The cruelty of some of them inspired the novelist Harriet Beecher Stowe to create the villain Simon Legree, a character in her novel *Uncle Tom's Cabin.*

Slave child. There was no one to care for young slaves, so they spent time in the fields from birth.

Auctioneer

Slave handler

Slave buyer

SLAVES FOR SALE

The Peculiar Institution was a business. Millions of dollars were made and spent on the sales of human beings each year until the end of the Civil War. This painting of a slave auction was made in 1852. The last public slave auction in the United States was held in St. Louis, Missouri, in 1865.

Overseer

Canvas cotton sack

KING COTTON

These are picked bolls of raw cotton. Until their tangled fibers are combed out and their seeds are removed, they cannot be woven into fabric. Slaves did these chores by hand until 1793. In that year, twenty-eight-year-old Eli Whitney of New England invented the cotton gin, a hand-cranked machine that combed and seeded cotton in large quantities. This made cotton the "king" of the Southern economy, allowed white planters to amass fortunes — and created a need for tens of thousands of slaves to work the cotton fields.

Cotton boll

The election of 1860

WHEN THE PRESIDENTIAL ELECTION of 1860 arrived, the candidates took positions on the great controversy of the day: where — and why — slavery should exist in the United States. John Bell, the little-known candidate of the Constitution Party, said slavery and the U.S. Constitution should be left as they were. The Democratic Party split into two factions at its convention. Pro-slavery Southerners nominated U.S. Vice President John C. Breckinridge of Kentucky as their candidate. Democrats who favored a compromise over the slavery issue named Illinois Senator Stephen Douglas as their candidate. The six-year-old Republican Party opposed slavery. Its candidate was Illinois attorney Abraham Lincoln, a man with little experience in government. Lincoln won the election, but with little popular support, because the majority had split its votes among the other three men. Opponents of the Republicans were outraged; some even demanded that the election be declared invalid, and repeated. Pro-slavery Americans were expected to accept quietly a leader they did not want. They took radical action instead.

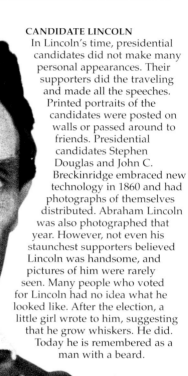

CANDIDATE LINCOLN
In Lincoln's time, presidential candidates did not make many personal appearances. Their supporters did the traveling and made all the speeches. Printed portraits of the candidates were posted on walls or passed around to friends. Presidential candidates Stephen Douglas and John C. Breckinridge embraced new technology in 1860 and had photographs of themselves distributed. Abraham Lincoln was also photographed that year. However, not even his staunchest supporters believed Lincoln was handsome, and pictures of him were rarely seen. Many people who voted for Lincoln had no idea what he looked like. After the election, a little girl wrote to him, suggesting that he grow whiskers. He did. Today he is remembered as a man with a beard.

A TOOL OF POLITICS
In the early and middle 1800s, supporters of all parties held rallies and parades for their candidates. Often these events took place at night, at the end of the workday. The item shown here is a parade torch. Dozens of marchers carried these flames to light the way for candidates, supporters, and marching bands as they walked through towns and villages chanting campaign slogans and singing campaign songs.

Angel of the Union, overlooking all

A WINNING PAIR
This Republican broadside, or poster, from 1860 features a portrait of Lincoln's running mate, U.S. Senator Hannibal Hamlin of Maine. As the Republican Party's vice-presidential candidate, Hamlin was expected to appeal to Northeastern voters. But the political climate changed over time. In 1864, the party replaced him with Andrew Johnson, a Union loyalist from Tennessee.

Symbol of Freedom

In the 1860 election, Douglas received 1,375,000 votes to Lincoln's 1,866,000. Eight months after the election, he became ill and died. In his last days, he asked all Americans to support Lincoln and the Union.

Symbol of Agriculture

Symbol of Industry

Symbol of Justice

LINCOLN.

HAMLIN.

CANDIDATE DOUGLAS
Senator Stephen Douglas was a famous politician in 1860. He was a skilled speaker and a likable man. Because of his slight stature, supporters called him the Little Giant. In 1858, Abraham Lincoln had run against him for his Senate seat, debating him in public several times. Although Lincoln lost that election, the debates popularized many of his views. They also served to introduce the little-known politician from Illinois to the broader American public.

CANDIDATE BRECKINRIDGE
Democrat John C. Breckinridge served as vice president during President James Buchanan's term in office. Buchanan was a Democrat from Pennsylvania, a free state. Breckinridge was a Democrat who came from Kentucky, a slave state. This combination of candidates from the North and the South had helped the Democratic Party win the White House in 1856. After losing the 1860 election, Breckinridge became a general in the Confederate army.

The Underground Railroad

A SLAVE STEALER'S HAND
Captain Jonathan Walker, an abolitionist seaman, was arrested at Key West, Florida, in the 1850s with a boatload of escaped slaves. He was jailed and branded on the palm of his right hand with the letters *SS*. The letters stood for "slave stealer." Abolitionists showed copies of this photograph at antislavery rallies throughout the North.

WHITE OPPONENTS of slavery, called abolitionists, organized their resistance in the 1820s and 1830s. Early leaders were clergymen and Quakers, members of a pacifist sect called the Society of Friends. One such leader was the Reverend Lyman Beecher, father of *Uncle Tom's Cabin* author Harriet Beecher Stowe. Another was Levi Coffin, a Quaker from North Carolina. Coffin left his home in 1826 and set up an operation in the free state of Ohio that became the Underground Railroad. This was a system of secret trails that ran from the northernmost slave states, through New England or the upper Midwest, to Canada. Escaped slaves linked up with guides, or "conductors," at locations they had heard about from other slaves. Conductors led the escapees along the trails and stopped to rest at "stations," the homes of abolitionists. One famous conductor was ex-slave Harriet Tubman. At its best, the Railroad liberated only about a thousand slaves a year. But its very existence, and the silent cooperation of thousands of Northerners, angered slave owners greatly. When antislavery militant John Brown led a terrorist raid on Harpers Ferry, Virginia, in 1859, pro-slavery Southerners felt their fears of the abolitionist movement were justified.

A STRATEGIC LOCATION
This landscape view of Harpers Ferry shows the importance of the town's location. Harpers Ferry lies at the northern end of the Shenandoah Valley, where the Shenandoah and Potomac Rivers meet. Because the community sits beside waters that could power machinery as well as serve as a natural roadway, it was chosen as the site for a U.S. government arsenal and arms factory. The location and the arsenal made Harpers Ferry a good target not only for John Brown in 1859, but also, two years later, for warring Civil War generals.

AN ABOLITIONIST FANATIC
John Brown was an unsuccessful leather tanner and farmer from Ohio. He moved to New York State and then Kansas, working for abolition. During the Kansas–Missouri border wars, he led others in the murder of some pro-slavery men. Then he traveled east, and in October, 1859, with the help of armed associates, attacked the town and government arsenal at Harpers Ferry. Brown hoped to arm slaves with guns from the arsenal and start a rebellion. He believed God wanted him to end slavery with bloodshed. After his arrest, he told his attorneys of this message. His words shocked them, and they wanted him to plead innocent by reason of insanity. Brown refused.

The Harpers Ferry engine house became a tourist attraction in the days following the crisis and was photographed often. This souvenir picture is from the postwar years.

JOHN BROWN'S FORT
When John Brown and his gang assaulted Harpers Ferry, they took several prominent citizens hostage. Armed with weapons taken from the town's federal arsenal, they barricaded themselves inside the local volunteer fire company's engine house and ignored the calls of local law enforcers to surrender. Within two days, a small force of U.S. Marines arrived and, using a ladder as a battering ram, smashed open the engine house door. All the Marines escaped harm, but Brown was wounded and arrested. He was tried, convicted of treason, and executed. After his death, John Brown became a martyr of the abolitionist movement.

A CHARISMATIC ABOLITIONIST

The best-known antislavery spokesperson of the prewar years was Frederick Douglass. He was the son of a Maryland plantation slave woman and her white master. During childhood, he was sent to live with a family in Baltimore. As a young man, he acquired forged papers, disguised himself as a seaman, and traveled north by railroad to freedom. After receiving an education, he became a forceful speaker on the abolitionist circuit and wrote a best-selling autobiography that described the heartbreak of slavery. When the Civil War ended, he won a post as a federal marshal in Washington, D.C., and continued campaigning for the rights of black Americans.

THE WOMAN CALLED MOSES

Harriet Tubman was a Maryland field slave who escaped to Philadelphia and became a famous conductor on the Underground Railroad. The more than three hundred slaves she led to freedom in the years before the Civil War nicknamed her Moses. John Brown knew her and called her General Tubman. By the time she was in her forties, she was a national celebrity. Tubman died in 1913, at the age of ninety-two, after living for many years in Auburn, New York, and working for the civil rights of black Americans. This painting was made in her later years.

A LIFE DEVOTED TO THE CAUSE OF FREEDOM

Sojourner Truth was born a slave in New York State around 1797. In 1827, she ran away from her master and took refuge with a New York abolitionist family named Van Wagener. She took their family name and supported herself by working as a domestic. In 1843, after claiming to have heard divine voices, she renamed herself Sojourner Truth and began lecturing on the cause of abolitionism. An illiterate, she dictated her life story to writer Olive Gilbert, and her book, *Narrative of Sojourner Truth*, became a best-seller in the years before the Civil War. The money she earned from her lectures and book sales helped support the work of the Underground Railroad. In the years following the war, Sojourner took up the cause of women's rights and continued her speaking career well into old age.

Secession

PRO-SLAVERY SOUTHERNERS were angry at the election of Abraham Lincoln to the presidency in 1860. Radicals among them believed they would no longer have a voice in American government. In South Carolina, where slaves outnumbered the white population, voters called for the state's secession from the Union. In December, 1860, a secession convention in the city of Charleston declared South Carolina's independence from the United States. Militiamen and citizens there seized U.S. government property. Major Robert Anderson took a small force into Fort Sumter, a brick fortification on a small island in the middle of Charleston Harbor. Anderson was determined to protect this bit of U.S. property from seizure. South Carolinians were equally determined to take the fort. Through January, February, and March, 1861, they surrounded the harbor with heavy cannons. Their guns prevented ships from bringing supplies to the fort. During this time, other states seceded. In March, in Montgomery, Alabama, these seceded states formed a new government, which was called the Confederate States of America. On April 11, Confederate cannons opened fire on Fort Sumter. These shots began the Civil War. Anderson's men fired back at the Charleston guns, but were forced to give in on April 12 when Confederate shells set their fort's interior on fire.

AN IMPORTANT HEADLINE
This headline from the *Charleston Mercury* is one of the most famous in U.S. history. It was issued as a one-sheet "extra" on December 20, 1860. The paper informed the people of Charleston of the vote for secession even before word of the event reached Washington, D.C.

THE GREAT SEAL OF THE CONFEDERACY
This is a pewter copy of the Great Seal of the Confederacy, the official stamp of the young Confederate government.

ALEXANDER STEPHENS, THE CONFEDERACY'S VICE PRESIDENT
The forgotten vice president of the Confederate States of America was Alexander Stephens of Georgia. Stephens was very thin, small, and sickly. He came to be known to the Confederate voters as Little Aleck.

PRESIDENT OF A REBEL NATION
In March, 1861, Jefferson Davis was named president of the Confederate States by convention delegates in Montgomery, Alabama. This was a temporary appointment. Later, in February, 1862, Davis stood for national election and was picked by the Southern people to serve a six-year term. This formal portrait of him was made long afterward. When first asked to serve as president, Davis said that he wanted to be a Confederate general instead. The future president of the Confederacy had served as a soldier during the Mexican War.

INSIDE CHARLESTON'S SECESSION HALL
Charleston citizens were jubilant when state representatives voted their state out of the Union. Both Northern and Southern newspapers covered celebrations at an auditorium called Institute Hall, where the vote was taken. The spot was later called Secession Hall.

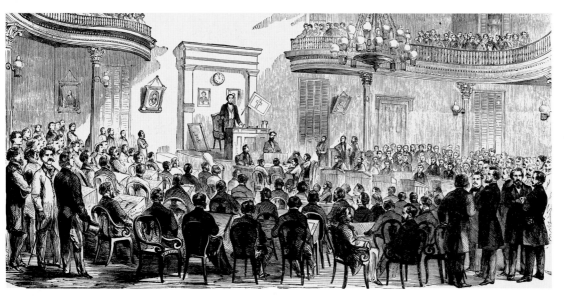

A RELIC OF THE FIGHT FOR FORT SUMTER

This cannonball was fired during the duel between Fort Sumter's cannons and Confederate guns in other forts around Charleston Harbor. Very little damage was done to Charleston during the fight, and no one on either side was killed by artillery fire.

Solid cast-iron ball

BEAUREGARD'S SOUVENIR

After the surrender of Sumter, Southerners commemorated the occasion by posing for photographs at the fort and by carrying away bits of the structure as mementos. A piece of the Union garrison's shattered flagstaff was cut, polished, and made into a walking stick for the leader of the Southern force there, General Pierre Gustave Toutant Beauregard.

A FLAG OF FORT SUMTER

This small flag flew over Sumter during its bombardment by Confederates. A Southern shell knocked it down early on April 12. Under fire, a Union sergeant climbed the flagpole and nailed it back into place.

This Confederate cannonball was intended for Fort Sumter. It landed in Charleston instead.

CANNONS FIRE ON FORT SUMTER

Troops led by General P.G.T. Beauregard fired on Fort Sumter at 4:30 A.M. on April 11, 1861. Major Robert Anderson, his eighty-five soldiers, and forty-three laborers fought back with forty-eight cannons. The federal flag was lowered on the afternoon of April 12. The next day, a formal surrender ceremony was held. The fort's defenders were then put on ships bound for New York City. There they were welcomed as heroes.

Raising armies

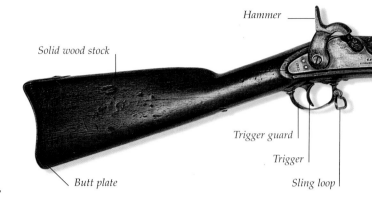

Hammer

Solid wood stock

Trigger guard

Trigger

Butt plate

Sling loop

APRIL 14, 1861, was a Monday. On this day, President Lincoln heard that Fort Sumter had surrendered. He issued a call for loyal state governors to send 75,000 militia troops to protect Washington, D.C., and put down the rebellion. Over the coming years, both Abraham Lincoln and Jefferson Davis asked for volunteers every few months. In 1862, the Confederate Congress approved conscription, the drafting of men into the army. The U.S. Congress did the same in 1863. Northern states also approved paying bounties, cash awards paid to men who volunteered to serve in some new regiments. Many Northerners and Southerners objected to the draft. There were draft riots in New York City in July, 1863. But in the end, both sides put millions of soldiers in the field. North Carolina provided more Confederate army regiments than any other Southern state. New York supplied the most Northern regiments.

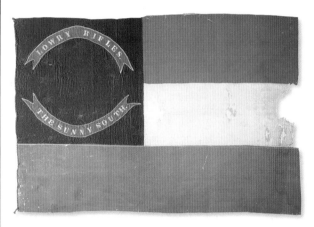

THE SUNNY SOUTH
Mississippi was the second state to secede. It sent 80,000 men into the army under its banners. This is the flag of one of the state's early volunteer units, the Lowry Rifles. Its men showed their regional pride by adopting the motto "The Sunny South" for their standard. After the initial patriotic rush of enlistments, however, it became harder and harder for the South to organize regiments like this one.

HOMEMADE UNIFORMS
Clothing hand made by folks at home was common wear in many of the first volunteer regiments. In the South, it was prevalent throughout the war. The sister of Private James Lampton of Mississippi made this hat for him out of pine straw.

THE 7TH NEW YORK GOES TO WAR
When Lincoln called for 75,000 troops, New York City sent its 7th Regiment of militia. Here, the people of the city cheer the regiment's men as they march to the train that will take them to Washington.

JOINING FOR BOUNTY MONEY
Many disliked the way some regiments recruited. These men are considering joining up. Among them are criminals called bounty jumpers. They will join, receive bounty money, then desert the army. Later, they will use an alias to join another regiment and receive more money.

Rear sight · **Barrel band** · **Forged steel barrel** · **Blade sight**

A STANDARD RIFLE
Both the Union and Confederate armies used versions of this .58 caliber rifle. In the North, it was called the Springfield Model 1861 for the Springfield, Massachusetts, armory where it was first made. The model shown here was made in Richmond, Virginia, for Southern troops.

Spout

Stamped tin

A RECRUITING POSTER
Before the invention of radio, television, and motion pictures, organizations and government officials spoke to individuals by using posters. These were hung in places where people often gathered, such as town squares, open-air markets, and the front of shops and newspaper offices. This enlistment poster was one of the most popular types seen in the first days of the Civil War. It does not mention pay or benefits. Rather, the picture of the patriotic soldier in battle gives recruits the impression that if they enlist, they will experience adventure.

VERY BASIC EQUIPMENT
Water was more important to the Civil War soldier than food and gunpowder. In summer, men were lost on marches because they suffered dehydration. Many of the first volunteers were given tin canteens, like this one, taken from U.S. government stockpiles.

Everyone's war

I<small>N THE</small> 1860<small>S</small>, some people were discouraged from joining the Union and Confederate armies due to old laws and traditions. Native Americans, for instance, were excluded from many volunteer regiments. In the Northeast, there was a great deal of prejudice against members of immigrant groups, and in many places they were also kept out of volunteer units. Men from all these minorities worked their way into the military in the same way: They formed their own volunteer regiments. Irishmen, Jews, Italians, and Germans enlisted in units made up of other patriotic immigrants. Native Americans fought in "Indian outfits" in both armies. The Benavides brothers from Texas raised a Confederate outfit made up of other Mexican Americans. The adventure of the Civil War also attracted professional soldiers from other countries, called foreign observers, who made themselves useful in battle. Some of them, such as Prussian army cavalry officer Heros Von Borke, who traveled with Robert E. Lee's Confederate army, actually went into combat.

ITALIAN VOLUNTEERS
Italian-born members of New York City's Garibaldi Guard wore uniforms that let everyone know their country of origin. Their broad-brimmed hats were decorated with rooster feathers. Such feathers are considered emblems of courage and are still worn on Italian military caps.

A LEADER IN BATTLE AND BUSINESS
Most members of the 120th Regiment of Ohio Volunteers were Protestant. However, their colonel, Marcus Spiegel, was a Jewish businessman who brought his leadership skills to the Union war effort. He and the 120th saw hard combat during the siege of Vicksburg, Mississippi. After the war, Spiegel became nationally known for his mail-order company.

IRISH TROOPS AT MASS
In the 1860s, most Americans were Protestant and were suspicious of different denominations and faiths. The Irish troops in this photograph had a Catholic priest as their chaplain. But members of one largely Jewish regiment in the Union army were not allowed to have a rabbi as their spiritual leader. The war was nearly over before the Northern army changed its rules and enlisted clergymen from certain ethnic and religious backgrounds.

Austro-Hungarian–style uniform coat

A MAN OF INFLUENCE
Before the war, Judah Benjamin was a U.S. senator from Louisiana. This photograph of him is from that period. Later, he served as the only Jewish member of Confederate President Jefferson Davis's cabinet. At different times, he was the Confederacy's attorney general and its secretary of state. He also served briefly as secretary of war. In that role, Benjamin's decisions affected the lives of all Confederate soldiers.

THE IRISHMAN FROM ARKANSAS
Patrick R. Cleburne was born in County Cork, Ireland. He studied pharmacy at school and later served for three years in Britain's Royal Army. After that, he immigrated to Arkansas and ran a drugstore. This background hid great military talent. In the Confederate army, he rose to the rank of major general and led his troops to many victories. Cleburne was killed in November, 1864, at the Battle of Franklin, near Nashville, Tennessee. He was shot while waving his military cap in the air and shouting for his men to follow him in a charge.

A TARGET FOR ENEMY FIRE
Irish-born Union Brigadier General Thomas F. Meagher raised a brigade of Irish immigrant volunteers. Each regiment in the brigade carried one of these banners. This flag of the brigade's 4th Regiment is the only one to survive the war. Because the green banners made good targets, they were shredded by Southern bullets.

Game of dominoes

Irish harp

A CHIEF AND A GENERAL
Stand Watie was a chief of the Cherokee tribe in what is today Oklahoma. He formed a brigade of Native Americans to fight for the South and was made a brigadier general. His troops fought at the battles of Wilson's Creek in Missouri and Pea Ridge in Arkansas. In June, 1865, Watie was the last Confederate general to surrender his troops.

EUROPEAN OBSERVERS
Civil War photographers liked to pose important visitors for pictures. Here are three titled French military men: from the left, the Duc de Chartes, the Prince de Joinville, and the Comte de Paris. They are all members of the same French titled family, and served with Union Major General George McClellan's staff in 1862.

Muzzle-loading rifle

Side knife

TWO GERMAN BROTHERS
The Midwest produced many regiments made up of men from Germany and Scandinavia. These two soldiers from Illinois, George and Herman Grothe, were both born in Germany.

Women at war

IN THE 1860S, AROUND THE GLOBE, laws and customs prohibited women from taking part in war. But in America there was a different attitude. For generations, women had endured the dangers of the frontier. They had supported their men in wars against the British, Mexicans, and Native Americans. In those conflicts, most soldiers were volunteers. When they went off to battle, they left the women behind to look after farms, businesses, and communities. At those times, women were often called on to bear the burden of "men's work" as well as the work traditionally considered their own. They proved they were tough. Men still did not want women to face flying bullets and cannon shot in the Civil War, but they did accept them taking part in war off the battlefield. Though their numbers were small, women played a role in support work in Union and Confederate government departments. Some were spies. While most army nurses were men, women were allowed to serve as hospital volunteers. Regiments of upper-class soldiers sometimes supported a vivandière, a uniformed female mascot who marched with the troops and performed camp chores. In the North, many women belonged to the Sanitary Commission. This was an organization that traveled to the field with supplies for soldier relief.

A CONFEDERATE ANGEL
Phoebe Pember is remembered for her selfless work in Confederate army hospitals around Richmond, Virginia. Mrs. Pember was a South Carolina widow. During the war, she kept a journal of her hospital experiences. Published after the conflict ended, it criticized the Southern government's administration and operation of its hospitals.

A UNION PATRIOT
Clara Barton is remembered as the founder of the American Red Cross. During the Civil War, she worked as a government clerk in Washington, D.C., then won fame as a battlefield nursing volunteer. In September, 1862, at the Battle of Antietam in Maryland, she came under hostile fire for the first time. Clara Barton frequently risked her life throughout the conflict while aiding the sick and wounded.

SUPPORTING THE TROOPS
These women are members of the Philadelphia Academy of Fine Arts. They are doing a traditional wartime task: sewing a flag for Union army volunteers.

Crutch

Medicine bottle

HOSPITAL NURSING
Northern female nursing volunteers were eventually organized by medical reformer Dorothea Dix. However, she prohibited them from serving near the front lines. Like the volunteer shown here, women who worked as nurses were confined to supervised service in hospitals. Male nurses bathed the patients and moved them; they also assisted doctors during grisly battlefield surgery.

A DUBIOUS SOLDIER
Loreta Janeta Velazquez was a Southerner of Cuban-American descent. She claimed she had donned a disguise and served in the Confederate army as Lieutenant Harry Buford so that she would be near her soldier-husband. She also claimed to have been widowed twice during the war and to have served as a spy. Most veterans found Madame Velazquez's claims outrageous. Yet the memoirs she wrote after the war, titled *The Woman in Battle,* sold well. Both of these portraits come from a copy of her book.

A GENUINE ARMY VOLUNTEER
Sarah Emma Edmonds was born in Canada, but was working in the United States when the Civil War broke out. Disguising herself as a man, she joined a Union army regiment and served without being detected until she became ill. Rather than have her gender discovered by an army doctor, Sarah Edmonds deserted. Following the war, she married, started a family, and became the only female member of the Grand Army of the Republic, a Union veterans' organization.

REFUGEES IN FLIGHT
When warring armies passed through communities, women and children often became refugees. The woman in this photograph with her wagon load of furniture and children was displaced when Union troops evicted all civilians from her county. Northerners used this strategy when they hunted guerrillas.

Furniture

Quilt

Sunbonnet

Gingham dress

The young and the old

THROUGHOUT HISTORY, there have been famous old soldiers and very brave, very young ones. When the Civil War first broke out, seventy-four-year-old Lieutenant General Winfield Scott led the Union army. He was in poor health, weighed more than three hundred pounds, and had trouble sitting on a horse. But before leaving the army in November, 1861, he developed a broad military strategy that later led to Union victory. For his part, John Clem of Ohio won national attention when, as a ten-year-old, he survived the vicious combat at the Battle of Shiloh, Tennessee, in April, 1862. He had forced himself on the men of the 22nd Michigan as their drummer boy. At Shiloh, enemy shell fragments smashed his little drum. Drawings of Clem appeared in newspapers, along with stories of his narrow escape, and made him a celebrity. But he was not the only extremely young volunteer. More than 3,900 boys aged sixteen and under wrangled their way into the Union army, and it is estimated that there were even more boy soldiers serving the Confederacy. Although soldiers in both armies were supposed to be between the ages of eighteen and forty-six, near the war's end, Southern states encouraged boys as young as fifteen to join the militia and pressed elderly men into military service.

THE WOUNDED DRUMMER BOY
This romanticized painting of a wounded young drummer being carried around the battlefield on the shoulder of an older soldier was popular in Northern homes in the years just after the war.

AN ELDERLY UNION VETERAN . . .
Winfield Scott was America's most honored soldier at the time the Civil War began. He joined the army in 1808, led troops in the War of 1812, commanded the American forces that conquered Mexico City in 1848, and was the Whig Party's presidential candidate in 1852. He was also the first military man to hold the rank of lieutenant general since George Washington. Scott was respected in the North for his loyalty. Though born and raised in slave-holding Virginia, he stood by the Union. He died in 1866 and is buried in New York State at the U.S. Army Military Academy at West Point.

. . . AND AN AGED CONFEDERATE GENERAL
Northerners called seventy-one-year-old David Twiggs a traitor. In 1861, Major General Twiggs, a native of Georgia, commanded the U.S. forces in Texas. When the Lone Star State seceded from the Union, he surrendered all U.S. forts in Texas to local Confederates and turned over all army supplies and payrolls to Southern authorities. His reward was a Confederate general's commission. However, his advanced age kept him from serving in the field. He died of natural causes in 1862 while the war was still under way.

The belt plate is the Georgia coat of arms.

Epaulet

What American boy today can imagine marching off to war with his father? This was not unheard of during the Civil War. Volunteers who made up the first militia companies came from small towns and neighborhoods. Often brothers or fathers and sons were among the members. This Southern parent and child posed for the camera in their dress militia uniforms before heading off for combat.

A BOY SOLDIER'S SOUVENIR

Landon Creek was very young when he joined a regiment of Mississippi volunteers. He was wounded three times before he turned fifteen. His war injuries inspired him to go back to school when peace came. He studied hard and became a doctor. But he always kept this small hat he had worn during the war to remind him of his days as a boy soldier.

White patent-leather cross belt

Gray wool tunic

Noncommissioned officer's dress sword

THE DRUMMER BOY OF SHILOH

John Clem ran away from his Ohio home to join the army at age nine. He had turned ten by the time he served at the Battle of Shiloh. The next year, in September, 1863, at the Battle of Chickamauga in Georgia, Clem shot a Southern officer who tried to force him to surrender. This won him even more celebrity. Years after the war, General Grant made him a lieutenant in the U.S. Army. John Clem retired as a major general in 1916.

NOT TOO YOUNG TO FIGHT

This unidentified Southern recruit is of school age. Many young boys scrawled the number 18 on a piece of paper, then stuffed the paper into the bottom of one of their shoes. When enlistment officers asked the youths if they were over eighteen, the underage volunteers believed that they could say "yes" without having lied since they were "over" the paper marked with "18."

Cap box

Outfitting armies

HOME AWAY FROM HOME
The waterproof leather knapsack was an item common to every foot soldier in the first years of the war. A leather-wrapped blanket roll was strapped to the top, and inside a soldier carried every bit of spare clothing he might have; his tin cup, plate, fork, and spoon; extra ammunition; and any personal items he might want to keep with him. As they lost more items and as regulations relaxed, many soldiers abandoned these sacks later in the war and took to carrying all their possessions in a simple blanket roll carried over their shoulders.

WHEN NATIONS GO TO WAR, they must make sure companies and factories produce clothing and equipment for their soldiers for as long as the fighting lasts. During America's Civil War, factories in the North did just that, producing blue wool uniforms, rifles, pistols, swords, ammunition, and camp equipment, as well as tools to repair all these things. To make the items quickly, they used standardized parts and many workers to mass-produce them. In the Confederate states, there were fewer factories and workers, so the South's fighting men often went into battle wearing homemade uniforms and carrying weapons imported from Europe or brought from arsenals in their hometowns. In the first years of the war, Southerners discovered their handmade clothing and imported rifles were just as good as those made in Northern factories. When these things wore out or broke, though, there was little or nothing with which to replace them. Many of the Confederate troops ended the war wearing rags and carrying weapons taken from Union army prisoners.

CONFEDERATE UNIFORMS APLENTY
At the start of the Civil War, many Southern troops wore attractive, sometimes fanciful uniforms. These pages from an 1861 copy of the illustrated newspaper *Harper's Weekly* show the variety of uniforms worn by some Confederate regiments. Most of these outfits were made by hometown tailors or the wives or mothers of the soldiers.

Canvas canteen cover

CARRYING FOOD AND DRINK
Infantrymen carried their water in canteens and personal items and some food rations in haversacks, bags slung across the shoulder on a strap. This canvas-covered canteen has a soldier's unit designation stenciled on it. Its cover could be soaked in water to keep the contents cool.

FOR CUT AND THRUST
This fighting blade, called a Model 1850, was carried by both Union and Confederate infantry officers. Southerners found great numbers of them stockpiled in local arsenals during the secession crisis. Many of these swords were carried throughout the conflict and were then taken home as souvenirs.

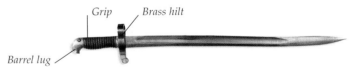

Grip   *Brass hilt*

Barrel lug

APPEARANCES ARE DECEIVING
Sword bayonets, copies of weapons made popular by foreign troops, were carried by some Northern and Southern regiments. While they looked frightening when attached to the end of a rifle, they were expensive to make and awkward to carry. Bayonets shaped like spikes replaced them.

Brass hand guard   *Hammer*   *Collapsing rear sight*   *Iron barrel*   *Front blade sight*

Trigger   *Sling loop*   *Sling loop*   *Ramrod*

Walnut shoulder stock

DEPENDABLE IN BATTLE
First called the Mississippi Rifle and later the Harpers Ferry Rifle, the single-shot muzzle-loading .54 caliber U.S. Model 1841 rifle was the standard weapon of the U.S. Army at the start of the Civil War. With a 33-inch barrel, it proved itself a potent weapon, firing a conical lead round called a minié bullet and finding its target at 1,000 yards. Once the fighting got rolling, however, it was replaced by the Model 1861 Springfield rifle-musket, which had a 40-inch barrel and threw a heavier caliber minié.

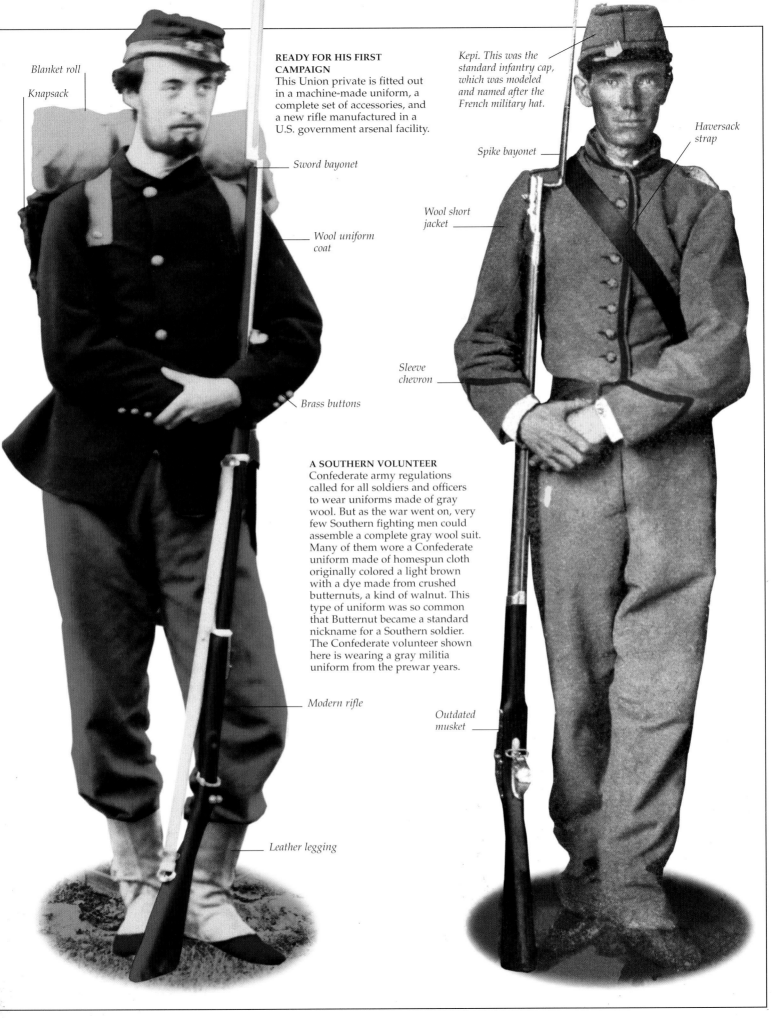

Blanket roll

Knapsack

READY FOR HIS FIRST CAMPAIGN
This Union private is fitted out in a machine-made uniform, a complete set of accessories, and a new rifle manufactured in a U.S. government arsenal facility.

Sword bayonet

Wool uniform coat

Brass buttons

Kepi. This was the standard infantry cap, which was modeled and named after the French military hat.

Haversack strap

Spike bayonet

Wool short jacket

Sleeve chevron

A SOUTHERN VOLUNTEER
Confederate army regulations called for all soldiers and officers to wear uniforms made of gray wool. But as the war went on, very few Southern fighting men could assemble a complete gray wool suit. Many of them wore a Confederate uniform made of homespun cloth originally colored a light brown with a dye made from crushed butternuts, a kind of walnut. This type of uniform was so common that Butternut became a standard nickname for a Southern soldier. The Confederate volunteer shown here is wearing a gray militia uniform from the prewar years.

Modern rifle

Outdated musket

Leather legging

Bull Run

Troops riding atop boxcars

TAKING THE TRAIN TO BATTLE
Troops led by Confederate General Joseph Johnston boarded railroad trains in Virginia's Shenandoah Valley and arrived at the Bull Run battlefield in time to reinforce Beauregard's forces. As the men were leaving the train station, some of the women who saw them off gave them gifts of treats for their journey.

NEAR WASHINGTON, D.C., is Manassas, Virginia. A stream nearby is named Bull Run. The fields around the stream were the sites of two large Civil War fights. The First Battle of Bull Run took place on July 21, 1861. At that time, Confederate General P.G.T. Beauregard commanded a 20,000-man army around Manassas that threatened the Union capital. President Lincoln sent Brigadier General Irvin McDowell with more than 30,000 troops to fight this force. Many of these men were ninety-day volunteers who were scheduled to be discharged in late July. As the troops maneuvered, several discharge dates arrived, and some of the soldiers went home. Many Washington-area residents wanted to see how the Union troops performed in combat, so they packed picnic lunches and rode out to the fields where the battle was expected. The fight started at dawn on July 21 and lasted through midafternoon. Both sides' soldiers were poorly trained, and in repeated attacks could not best one another. But Beauregard's men received reinforcements, who helped drive the Union soldiers from the field. As they retreated, they were shelled. This frightened the civilians, and they clogged the roads as they fled. This, in turn, created a traffic jam that panicked the Northern troops. Many dropped their weapons and ran for the safety of the Washington defenses.

THE COMMANDER OF THE UNION FORCES
General Irvin McDowell is the tall, heavyset officer in this photograph. Bull Run was the only large-scale battle where McDowell commanded the Union forces. Later in 1861, George McClellan, the man standing to McDowell's left, would lead the Northern army.

A limber, a field artillery ammunition chest

Gray uniform

Blanket roll

Sword bayonet

Union volunteer of the 7th New York Regiment

Garibaldi Guard member in an Italian army hat

New York volunteer of the Fire Zouave Regiment

Legging

AN ASSORTMENT OF UNIFORMS
Clothing was a problem for both armies at Bull Run. Many volunteers showed up to fight dressed in uniforms that neither side recognized. Some Northerners wore gray uniforms. Some Southerners wore blue uniforms. Others, such as men who joined Zouave regiments, wore gaudy outfits. The Zouaves took their name and flamboyant clothing from French regiments that, in turn, had modeled their uniforms on the clothes of fighters of the Zouava tribe of Algeria in Africa. The lack of standard military dress created deadly confusion on the battlefield.

Newspaper artist

One of many who fought in shirtsleeves

Irish flag of the 69th New York

Havelock, a covering worn as protection from the sun

National flag of the Confederacy

Knapsack

Iron bayonet

AMATEUR SOLDIERS CHARGE

These are the men of the 69th New York, a group of volunteer soldiers. Many of them were Irish immigrants. They carried a green flag with an Irish harp symbol stitched on it. The 69th's colonel, Michael Corcoran (on the horse), was captured during this battle. He was later exchanged for Confederate prisoners and became a brigadier general.

THE LEADER OF THE CONFEDERATE TROOPS

General P.G.T. Beauregard led the main Confederate army in the First Battle of Bull Run. Here he is wearing his old U.S. Army uniform. Most of his prewar experience involved army engineering projects, not combat. However, his success in capturing Fort Sumter in April, 1861, led to Beauregard's being appointed one of the highest-ranking generals of the Confederacy.

General's stars

COMMANDER BEAUREGARD'S EPAULETS

These brass epaulets were worn on the shoulders of General Beauregard's dress uniform. They were stored in a large hard leather case when not being worn.

Civilian

UNION VOLUNTEERS MARCH TO BATTLE

Brigadier General Irvin McDowell's men march to the sound of the guns. In this newspaper drawing done on-site, civilians are seen talking to and distracting some of the officers. The presence of townspeople at the battle caused problems and confusion for the soldiers.

RACING AWAY FROM DEFEAT

After the war, an artist made this painting of the panic that ensued during the Union army's retreat from Bull Run. The excitement began when a Confederate shell hit Union wagons on a narrow bridge and blocked the way. Union soldiers felt trapped. Instead of marching away from the battlefield in an orderly way, they threw down their equipment and ran desperately for their lives.

The sick and wounded

IF A CIVIL WAR SOLDIER BECAME SICK or was hurt in battle, he was in serious trouble. In the 1860s, there were no medicines to fight infections — no one had heard of germs. The bullets fired by Civil War rifles were very heavy and powerful. They often smashed the arm or leg bones of gunshot victims. Doctors could not repair those bone injuries, so they usually cut off a damaged limb to save the patient. The only painkillers available for this surgery were chloroform, ether, or whiskey. If a wound became infected, hospital workers encouraged flies to lay their eggs in it. They hoped the creatures that came out of the newly hatched fly eggs — maggots — would eat the diseased flesh. Miraculously, this cure sometimes worked. But more soldiers were killed by camp illnesses than by battle wounds. Polluted drinking water gave troops diphtheria and cholera. In those days, the only treatment for these diseases was doses of the narcotic opium. This drug eased the victim's intestinal distress and kept him from dying of dehydration. Just the same, tens of thousands of men died of these diseases as well as of measles, mumps, malaria, and yellow fever. The causes of and cures for these illnesses would not be discovered for several decades.

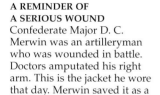

A REMINDER OF A SERIOUS WOUND
Confederate Major D. C. Merwin was an artilleryman who was wounded in battle. Doctors amputated his right arm. This is the jacket he wore that day. Merwin saved it as a souvenir, along with a pair of left-handed gloves given to him by his sympathetic men. Like many other soldiers, he fought on through the war despite his disability.

A MEDICAL MAN'S UNIFORM
This is the homespun "butternut" uniform of Confederate Major William H. Harrison. His records describe him as the medical purveyor of the South's Army of Tennessee. This is believed to mean he provided that army with medical supplies. Union army medical officers' uniforms were distinguished by black stripes down the outside pants seams.

PART-TIME AMBULANCE WORKERS
In both the Union and Confederate armies, cooks and musicians worked as stretcher bearers during battles. In this photograph of Union Zouave troops performing an ambulance drill, the discarded drum hints that these men made music when not carrying the wounded. Their ambulance had few springs, so its bumpy ride was painful for its injured passengers.

Zouave turban *Litter or stretcher* *Straps for hanging stretchers* *Rolled canvas awning*

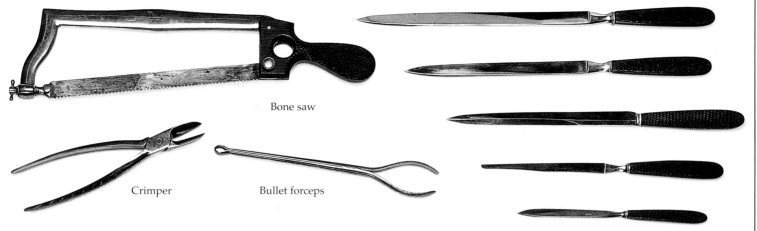

Bone saw

Amputation knives

A WARTIME SURGEON'S INSTRUMENTS

A bullet forceps, used to extract bullets, a crimper for snipping off bits of shattered bone, and a bone saw were the tools surgeons used most after battles. The most common operation that an army surgeon performed was an amputation. Amputation knives came in a variety of sizes. They enabled the surgeon to remove anything he needed to, from the tip of a little finger to an entire leg.

Crimper

Bullet forceps

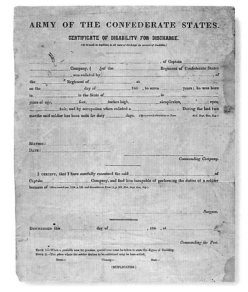

ARMY OF THE CONFEDERATE STATES.

CERTIFICATE OF DISABILITY FOR DISCHARGE.

AN HONORABLE DISCHARGE

When a soldier was too sick or hurt to continue serving in the army, a doctor filled out a certificate of disability. This form indicated that the trooper was being honorably discharged, and prevented the disabled man from being conscripted back into the service.

Zouave drum

NEXT-TO-LAST RESTING PLACES

Many Northern and Southern soldiers died in army hospitals. Because the railroads were busy with other war concerns, often the bodies were not immediately sent home for burial. This photograph of temporary graves outside a Union army hospital at City Point, Virginia, shows where some of these deceased men were laid to rest. When the war ended, many of these bodies were exhumed and shipped home for final burial.

A RIGHT-ARMED GENERAL . . .

Union General Philip Kearny was a professional soldier who had lost his left arm in combat before the Civil War. As his photograph shows, he is armed with a sword and ready for a fight. He was one of many officers who continued to serve even though they had lost an arm, a leg, or an eye.

One white dress glove

French-style kepi

. . . AND A GENERAL WITH A LEFT ARM

Union General Oliver O. Howard lost his right arm in action. General Kearny, missing his left arm, visited Howard in the hospital and consoled him with a joke, saying that now they could buy gloves together. Howard soldiered on through the war and later founded a college for black Americans, Howard University in Washington, D.C.

Great commanders

Confederate general's stars

JOSEPH E. JOHNSTON
Johnston was a U.S. Army brigadier general who joined Southern service to lead Jefferson Davis's troops in Virginia. Later, he fought at Atlanta and was the man who surrendered the Army of Tennessee to General Sherman in spring, 1865.

Grant's war horse Cincinnati

SOME OF THE BEST-KNOWN SOLDIERS and sailors in American history earned their reputations in the Civil War. A few were famous before the conflict, and a few also continued to make history after it. Confederate General Robert E. Lee's name was newsworthy as early as the Mexican War, when, as a U.S. Army officer, he scouted out the route the Americans used to fight their way to Mexico City. Philip Sheridan, a Union cavalry general, was known for several Civil War victories and won fame again as an Indian fighter years later. Several military men were also known for making tough personal choices when the war started. Many Southern commanders, such as Lee and Joseph Johnston, gave up power and position in the U.S. armed forces to serve the Confederacy. Others found opportunity. Union General U. S. Grant was a poor store clerk before the war. The conflict gave him a chance to show he could be a leader.

Lieutenant general's stars

U. S. GRANT
Before the war, Ulysses S. Grant of Illinois considered himself a failure. After a West Point education, he tried army life, left that to try business, and ended up impoverished. But his military training won him the rank of Union army colonel in the war's first days. Early success earned him promotions. After his victory in April, 1862, at the Battle of Shiloh in Tennessee, he was given greater responsibilities. He was later named general in chief of all Union armies and defeated Robert E. Lee's army in April, 1865. His fame helped win him the U.S. presidency in 1868. Today he is honored with a portrait on the $50 bill.

STONEWALL JACKSON
Born Thomas Jackson, this Southern general was a professor at the Virginia Military Institute when the Civil War began. He won his nickname, Stonewall, for his tough action as an officer at the First Battle of Bull Run. He won his fame as an expert in strategy and tactics and for victories in the Shenandoah Valley. Jackson was also a victim of bad luck. In May, 1863, he was wounded by North Carolina troops in an accident at the Battle of Chancellorsville, Virginia, and died several days later.

GEORGE B. McCLELLAN
George Brinton McClellan led the Union's Army of the Potomac through the Battle of Antietam, Maryland, in September, 1862. After that inconclusive fight, he was fired by President Lincoln. He ran against Lincoln as the Democratic Party's presidential candidate in 1864. Following the war, he was governor of New Jersey.

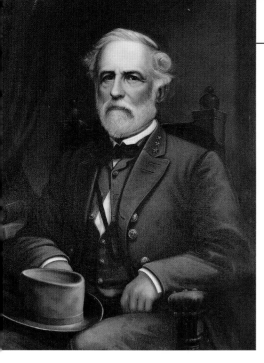

WILLIAM T. SHERMAN

William Tecumseh Sherman had been a peacetime army officer and had tried jobs in business and education before the war. From the Battle of Shiloh onward, he was U. S. Grant's friend and comrade. He is remembered for burning Atlanta and for desolating the state of Georgia on a campaign called the March to the Sea.

Sherman's war horse Lexington

ROBERT E. LEE

Robert E. Lee was the son of Revolutionary War hero "Light Horse" Harry Lee. As a young man, he married into the Custis clan, the stepfamily of President George Washington. Nationally known for his 1859 capture of abolitionist fanatic John Brown, he turned down an offer to lead the Union's largest army in 1861, and instead remained loyal to his home state of Virginia. Today Lee's prewar estate is the site of the famed national military cemetery, Arlington.

J.E.B. STUART

James Ewell Brown Stuart led Robert E. Lee's cavalry corps until mortally wounded at the Battle of Yellow Tavern, Virginia, in 1864. He was famous in the North and South as a flamboyant soldier who took great chances.

RAPHAEL SEMMES

Confederate Admiral Raphael Semmes was known to some as the Pirate Semmes. He was a veteran sailor who commanded commerce raiders, vessels that attacked Union merchant ships around the globe. This challenged the rules of warfare and made Semmes known everywhere. After the war, he refused to return to the United States and lived in England.

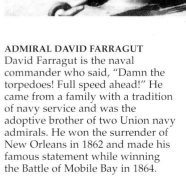

Admiral's rank insignia

Cuff braid indicating rank

PHILIP SHERIDAN

Sheridan was a professional soldier and the Union's most successful cavalry commander. After seeing military action in the Kansas-Missouri border wars, he led Civil War infantry. He was promoted and took command of the army's cavalry in Virginia. As a cavalry leader, he helped defeat Robert E. Lee at Appomattox.

ADMIRAL DAVID FARRAGUT

David Farragut is the naval commander who said, "Damn the torpedoes! Full speed ahead!" He came from a family with a tradition of navy service and was the adoptive brother of two Union navy admirals. He won the surrender of New Orleans in 1862 and made his famous statement while winning the Battle of Mobile Bay in 1864.

Arming soldiers

THE FIRST CIVIL WAR VOLUNTEERS carried a variety of blades and firearms. Their generals urged them to accept standard weapons that any soldier could use. The rifles they preferred were single-shot arms loaded at the muzzle. They fired a cone-shaped lead slug called a minié. The slug or bullet came wrapped in paper. A premeasured amount of gunpowder also came in the paper package. To load this rifle, a soldier pulled one of these cartridges from a box on his belt. He tore open the bottom of the cartridge with his teeth and poured the gunpowder down the muzzle of the rifle. Next he placed the bullet in the muzzle. Pulling a long metal rod called a ramrod from its place under the rifle's barrel, the soldier then rammed the bullet firmly down to the bottom of the barrel. To fire the rifle, he placed a metal cap filled with explosive on a metal piece called a nipple. When he cocked back the rifle's hammer and pulled its trigger, the hammer hit the cap and fired the weapon.

BOWIE KNIFE
Bowie knives had blades as long as a man's forearm and were carried by many Civil War soldiers. They were made famous on the American frontier and were named for their inventor, Jim Bowie, a Texas patriot who fought at the Alamo. The Bowie knife shown here with its red leather sheath was made in Sheffield, England, and was carried by a Southern soldier.

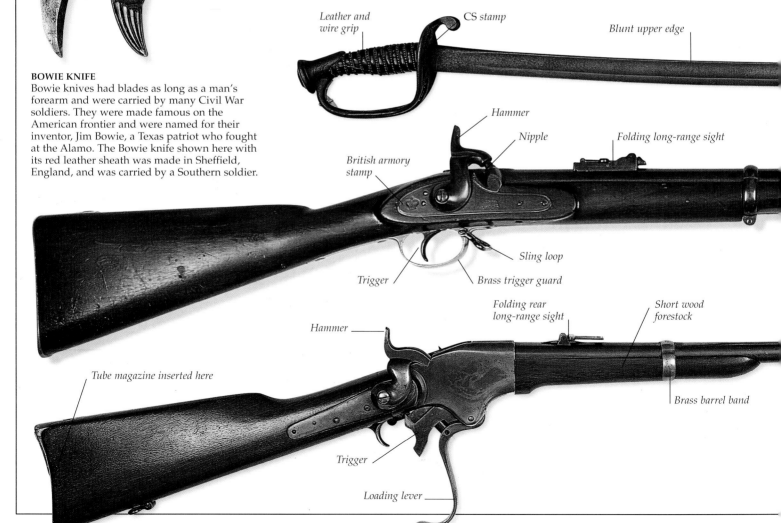

Leather and wire grip

CS stamp

Blunt upper edge

Hammer

Nipple

Folding long-range sight

British armory stamp

Trigger

Sling loop

Brass trigger guard

Folding rear long-range sight

Short wood forestock

Hammer

Tube magazine inserted here

Brass barrel band

Trigger

Loading lever

TROOPS WITH HENRY RIFLES

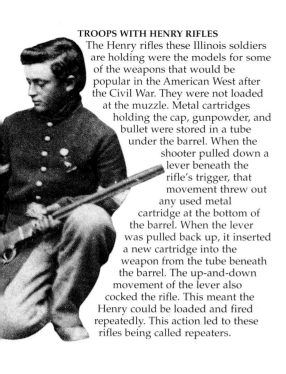

The Henry rifles these Illinois soldiers are holding were the models for some of the weapons that would be popular in the American West after the Civil War. They were not loaded at the muzzle. Metal cartridges holding the cap, gunpowder, and bullet were stored in a tube under the barrel. When the shooter pulled down a lever beneath the rifle's trigger, that movement threw out any used metal cartridge at the bottom of the barrel. When the lever was pulled back up, it inserted a new cartridge into the weapon from the tube beneath the barrel. The up-and-down movement of the lever also cocked the rifle. This meant the Henry could be loaded and fired repeatedly. This action led to these rifles being called repeaters.

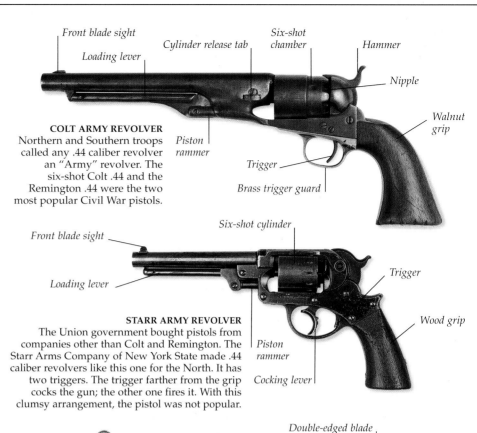

Front blade sight

Loading lever

Cylinder release tab

Six-shot chamber

Hammer

Nipple

Walnut grip

Piston rammer

Trigger

Brass trigger guard

COLT ARMY REVOLVER

Northern and Southern troops called any .44 caliber revolver an "Army" revolver. The six-shot Colt .44 and the Remington .44 were the two most popular Civil War pistols.

Front blade sight

Loading lever

Six-shot cylinder

Trigger

Wood grip

Piston rammer

Cocking lever

STARR ARMY REVOLVER

The Union government bought pistols from companies other than Colt and Remington. The Starr Arms Company of New York State made .44 caliber revolvers like this one for the North. It has two triggers. The trigger farther from the grip cocks the gun; the other one fires it. With this clumsy arrangement, the pistol was not popular.

CONFEDERATE FOOT OFFICER'S SWORD

Southern factories made swords for Confederate infantry officers. The sword here is modeled on one that had been made for U.S. Army infantry officers for years before the Civil War began. The letters *CS* are stamped on the outside of the sword's brass hand guard.

Double-edged blade

Double-edged tip

ARTILLERYMAN'S SHORT SWORD

Long before the Civil War, the U.S. Army gave soldiers who fired cannons these short swords. They were modeled on the swords carried by soldiers in the army of ancient Rome. American artillerymen were expected to use these blades to defend themselves and their cannons. By the time the Civil War broke out, however, these swords were not the best weapons. Soldiers used them instead as tools for cutting rope and cannon fuses.

Steel barrel band

Sling loop

Metal ramrod

ENFIELD RIFLE

Southern soldiers used the same rifles as Union infantry. They also used the Enfield, a .577 caliber weapon imported from Great Britain. It was marked by a crown or tower symbol stamped into the metal near the hammer. The stamp meant it had been made in England's Royal Armoury.

Cup to create a hollow base in a bullet

Molten lead poured here

Enfield bullet mold

Cleaning tool

PERCUSSION CAPS

These brass caps are filled with a small amount of explosive. They fit on a metal nipple underneath a rifle's hammer or at the end of a revolver's cylinder. Soldiers carried a supply of caps in a separate small box on their belts.

Explosive fulminate of mercury

Worm screw, which attaches to a ramrod to remove stuck bullets from a barrel

Nipple wrench

Stamped brass cap

BULLET MOLD AND RIFLE TOOLS

To make bullets, a thin lead bar was put into a pot and then set atop a fire. When the lead turned to liquid, it was poured into a bullet mold. After the lead cooled and hardened, the handles of the mold were pulled apart and the newly made bullet was pulled out. The other items here are tools that could be attached to a ramrod and used to clean a rifle barrel or remove a jammed bullet from it.

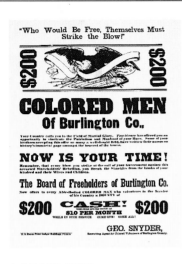

A CALL TO ARMS
Many Northern communities wanted to raise units of black volunteers, but not all of them had large black populations. Posters were displayed throughout whole counties in hopes of raising a full hundred-man company.

Black volunteers

THE GOVERNMENT TOOK A CENSUS the year before the Civil War. It showed there were fewer than 500,000 "free Negroes" in the United States. But there were almost 4 million blacks held in slavery. After the war started, the U.S. Congress did not allow free blacks or escaped slaves to join the Union army. Then President Lincoln issued his final Emancipation Proclamation in January, 1863. The decree stated that all slaves living in Confederate states were to be considered free. This document encouraged Congress to pass a law allowing black men to volunteer for Union military service. Soon there were close to 200,000 blacks serving in the Northern army and navy. These men were paid less than white soldiers and were often given worn uniforms and poor equipment. They could not become officers. If they were captured, they were shot or enslaved. However, these risks did not stop black men from taking part in combat. Several black soldiers won the Union's highest award for bravery, the Medal of Honor.

FLAGS FOR A BLACK REGIMENT
Black regiments were called U.S. Colored Troops, or U.S.C.T. for short. When they were presented with flags to carry off to war, there was often a large ceremony. Here, the men of the 20th U.S.C.T. are given flags in front of a cheering New York City crowd in 1864. These were proud patriotic moments. When regiments returned from the war, their flags were displayed in places of honor by the state and federal governments.

FIGHTING MEN
Some prejudiced Northerners believed that black volunteers could do heavy labor and small tasks in the army, but they were not sure these volunteers would fight. When given the chance, though, black fighting men proved their bravery in combat. Many posed for photographs like this one, demonstrating that they had combat training and fighting skills.

A SLAVE HERO
Robert Smalls was a slave who worked around Confederate Navy vessels in Charleston, South Carolina. One day he hijacked a ship loaded with new Confederate cannons. Also onboard were Smalls's wife and children, as well as several slave friends and their families. Smalls turned the Southern ship and its cargo of guns over to the Union navy and was rewarded. He, his family, and the others were also freed from slavery. Smalls's act of daring made him famous in the North. Following the war, he was elected to the U.S. House of Representatives. This photograph is from the postwar years.

A REJECTED VOLUNTEER
Attitudes about race were not the same all over the South. In lower Louisiana, for instance, there had been a tradition of black military service already. Free black volunteers had fought to defend the city of New Orleans during the War of 1812. When the Civil War broke out, free New Orleans blacks raised the Louisiana Native Guards regiment and volunteered to defend their city once again. Some, like this regiment member, even had their photographs taken in uniform. But the government of the Confederacy could not overcome its racial prejudice. It would not allow the Native Guards into its army.

Canvas four-man tent

Main camp

Mattross, a wood piece used to move a carriage tail

Rammer

PROUD BLACK CANNONEERS

Not long before posing with their cannon, these black artillerymen were slaves. They were among thousands of escaped slaves who were organized into army regiments late in the war. Many of them could neither read nor write. Because of this, they were trained by white troopers or officers, who read aloud to them from military manuals and then drilled them repeatedly. In this way, these blacks were able to memorize great amounts of material, and many of them became crack soldiers.

Colonel Robert Gould Shaw

THE BRAVEST BLACK REGIMENT

Early in 1863, Massachusetts governor John Andrew authorized the recruitment of an all-black regiment from his state. He also selected Robert Gould Shaw, the son of a prominent white family of abolitionists, to lead it. In July, 1863, the regiment, named the 54th Massachusetts, was asked to charge heavily armed Confederates dug in at Fort Wagner, outside Charleston, South Carolina. Colonel Shaw, with sword and pistol in hand, led the regiment's attack and was the first to reach the top of the fort's walls. He was killed there as he shouted, "Onward, Fifty-fourth!" The attack failed and cost the regiment 272 troopers in addition to Shaw. Intending to insult the memory of the white colonel, Confederates buried him in a mass grave along with his dead black soldiers. Shaw and the 54th are memorialized with a sculpture in Boston's Public Gardens.

FROM SLAVE TO SOLDIER

This photograph of a young black Union army drummer named Jackson was circulated all across the North, together with a photograph of the same young man dressed in the rags he had been wearing when he showed up behind Union lines as an escaped slave. Some white Northerners doubted that former slaves could be turned into disciplined soldiers. The pair of photographs were shown to convince those doubters that slaves could be trained to fight for the freedom of others in bondage.

The horsemen

THE AMERICAN CIVIL WAR was the last large conflict in world history in which soldiers on horseback played an important part. Cavalrymen scouted out the positions and movements of enemy armies. They made shock attacks — the famous cavalry charges that could break up infantry formations. If an enemy army retreated, cavalry troops were expected to pursue and harass it. Additionally, horse soldiers were used as speedy messengers and as armed escorts for prisoners or traveling dignitaries. Within decades, the armies of the world gradually turned over these cavalry jobs to telephones, automobiles, tanks, and biplanes. But in the 1860s, the horse soldiers of the Union and Confederate armies saw themselves as mounted knights. Many Southern cavalrymen dressed in flashy uniforms, some wearing wide hats with large ostrich plumes. Both Northern and Southern horsemen wore tall leather boots and carried sabers as well as pistols and carbines.

Colt revolver

18-gauge shotgun barrel

LeMat revolver

CAVALRY REVOLVERS AND HOLSTER
The .44 caliber Colt revolver was one of the most common Civil War cavalry weapons. It was meant to be carried in a leather holster like the one shown here, on the left side of a trooper's belt. The LeMat revolver fired nine .40 caliber slugs. It also featured a short second barrel that fired an 18-gauge shotgun round. These pistols were made in France and imported by the Confederate government. Southern cavalry leader General J.E.B. Stuart carried a LeMat.

A MISSISSIPPI HORSE SOLDIER
Soldiers often tried to look serious or warlike in photographs. The Mississippi trooper in this image does that by showing the camera one of his cavalry weapons. He is holding a six-shot black powder revolver.

Bit

Halter

SABERS OF THE NORTH AND SOUTH
The heavy, curved blade of a saber was the symbol of cavalry service around the world. The U.S. Army Model 1850 saber was carried by both Northern and Southern troopers during the Civil War. Because of its weight and length, professional soldiers called it the Old Wrist Breaker. Confederate factories produced thousands of copies of it for Southern horsemen to carry into battle.

Leather and wire grip

Hilt

Model 1850 saber

Hilt hook to catch and turn away an enemy blade

Confederate saber

Sharpened upper edge

Pommel   *Hand guard*

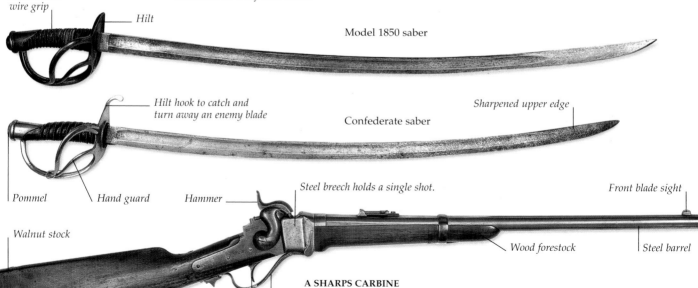

Hammer

Steel breech holds a single shot.

Front blade sight

Walnut stock

Wood forestock   *Steel barrel*

A SHARPS CARBINE
The .52 caliber Sharps carbine was a favorite of Union cavalrymen. It had a 22-inch barrel and was a single-shot weapon. It was not a muzzle loader. Its trigger guard was also a loading lever. When pulled down, the lever opened a slot near the hammer, where a paper or linen cartridge was inserted. This allowed soldiers to load and fire it about eight times a minute. After the war, the Sharps remained popular as a hunting weapon and was often called a buffalo gun.

Trigger

Steel trigger guard and loading lever, which pulls down to open the breech

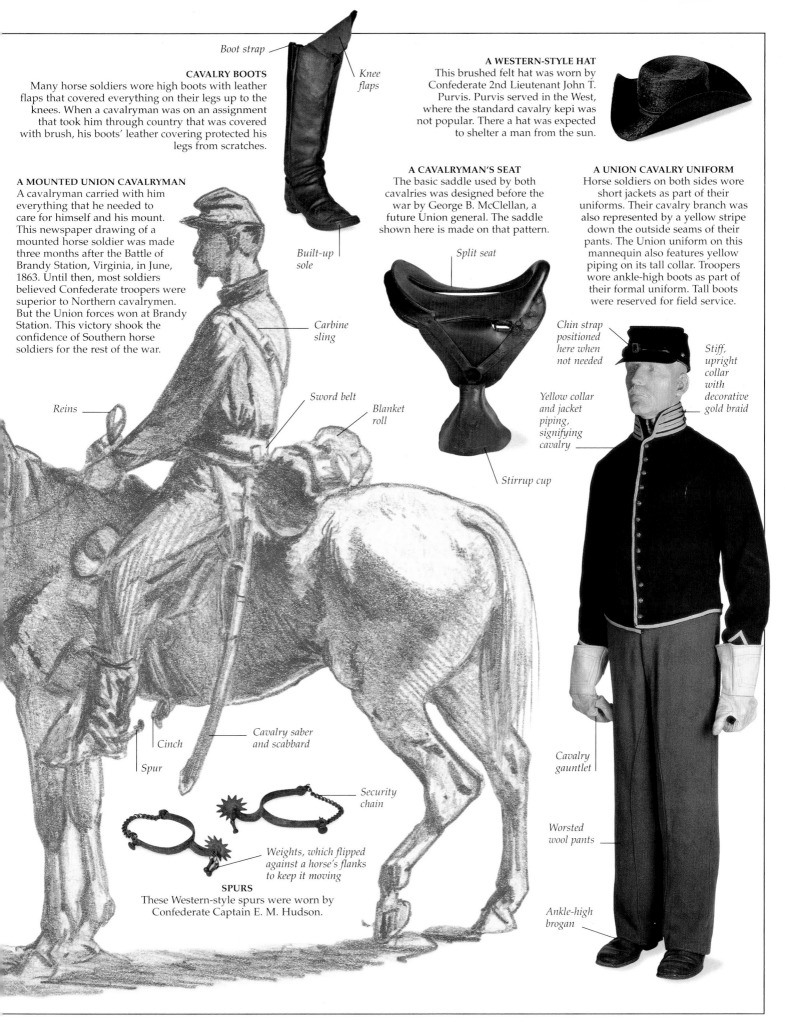

CAVALRY BOOTS

Many horse soldiers wore high boots with leather flaps that covered everything on their legs up to the knees. When a cavalryman was on an assignment that took him through country that was covered with brush, his boots' leather covering protected his legs from scratches.

Boot strap

Knee flaps

Built-up sole

A WESTERN-STYLE HAT

This brushed felt hat was worn by Confederate 2nd Lieutenant John T. Purvis. Purvis served in the West, where the standard cavalry kepi was not popular. There a hat was expected to shelter a man from the sun.

A MOUNTED UNION CAVALRYMAN

A cavalryman carried with him everything that he needed to care for himself and his mount. This newspaper drawing of a mounted horse soldier was made three months after the Battle of Brandy Station, Virginia, in June, 1863. Until then, most soldiers believed Confederate troopers were superior to Northern cavalrymen. But the Union forces won at Brandy Station. This victory shook the confidence of Southern horse soldiers for the rest of the war.

Carbine sling

Reins

Sword belt

Blanket roll

A CAVALRYMAN'S SEAT

The basic saddle used by both cavalries was designed before the war by George B. McClellan, a future Union general. The saddle shown here is made on that pattern.

Split seat

Stirrup cup

A UNION CAVALRY UNIFORM

Horse soldiers on both sides wore short jackets as part of their uniforms. Their cavalry branch was also represented by a yellow stripe down the outside seams of their pants. The Union uniform on this mannequin also features yellow piping on its tall collar. Troopers wore ankle-high boots as part of their formal uniform. Tall boots were reserved for field service.

Chin strap positioned here when not needed

Stiff, upright collar with decorative gold braid

Yellow collar and jacket piping, signifying cavalry

Cinch

Cavalry saber and scabbard

Spur

Security chain

Weights, which flipped against a horse's flanks to keep it moving

SPURS

These Western-style spurs were worn by Confederate Captain E. M. Hudson.

Cavalry gauntlet

Worsted wool pants

Ankle-high brogan

Army camp life

CIVIL WAR SOLDIERS SPENT almost all their time outdoors, in every season of the year. When traveling on campaigns, most men slept in bivouac, meaning they simply lay down on the ground and covered themselves with blankets. Troops assigned duty in and around cities sometimes lived in barracks, simple wood buildings. But when assigned to large camps, the troops slept in tents that held from four to eight men. They ate meals prepared by army cooks who worked out of large tent kitchens with portable ovens. The soldiers spent their days practicing drills, doing chores, and repairing worn equipment. In their limited free time, they wrote letters home, read, gambled, had their likenesses made by photographers, or enjoyed concerts by their units' marching bands. Fighting was not common in winter, and the men often built simple cabins to keep themselves warm at that cold time of year. In the spring, these huts became firewood.

OUTSIDE THE BARRACKS
In this 1861 photograph, Union troops pose in front of and on top of their barracks. Signs on the walls indicate the men belong to their regiment's Company I. The soldiers in front are playing cards with the company drummer.

Bass saxhorn

Musician's sword

PARADE
POLKA MARCH,
AS PLAYED BY THE
N. O. Washington Artillery Band.

MAKING MUSIC
These are members of a Union army marching band. Each man holds a marching band instrument now extinct, the saxhorn. Because the bell of the horn lay back across the musician's shoulder, the tune could be heard by the troops behind. The cover sheet is for a lively military number that was made popular by the Confederate army's Washington Artillery Band of New Orleans.

THE DEVIL'S PLAYTHINGS
Card playing became a huge camp fad in both armies, even when the men had nothing to bet with except uniform buttons. But many soldiers would throw away their cards before going into battle. If they were killed in the fight, they did not want their relatives to know they had been pursuing the "sin" of gambling.

SET FOR DINNER
Both Union and Confederate troops ate off tin plates and drank from tin cups. The plate shown here comes with a unique folding fork, spoon, knife combination, an item guaranteed to take up little room in a soldier's crowded knapsack.

Tin plate

Combination fork, spoon, knife

Hardtack

WINTER'S COLD
A Confederate soldier painted this scene of his army in "winter quarters," the time when troops built crude huts and cabins to stave off the cold. The painting shows that some men even installed chimneys, which allowed them to build warmth-giving fires inside.

WRITING HOME
In these years before electronic communication, a letter was the quickest way for a soldier to get a message home. Telegraphic messages were expensive and, during the war, controlled by the military. These are some writing implements of a Union soldier, as well as a letter, some patriotic stationery, and a rolled-up lap desk. The desk is made from small slats of wood. When it was unrolled, the desk provided a smooth writing surface for a soldier seated on the ground.

SOMEBODY'S DARLING
During the Civil War, soldiers started a practice that continues to this day: carrying photographs of their faraway wives and children with them. This photograph of a Southern soldier's little girl was carried in a hinged leather case and held in place with a brass frame.

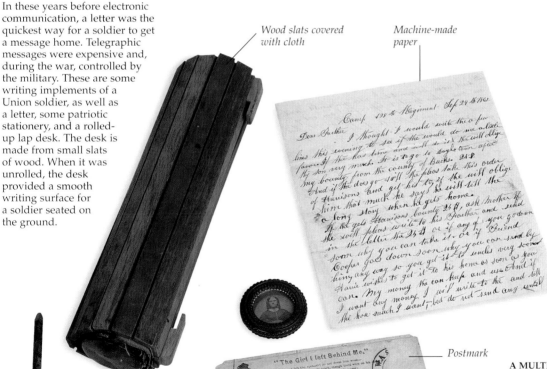

Wood slats covered with cloth

Machine-made paper

Postmark

Patriotic envelope

Pen nibs

Opening slides over barrel

Three-sided spike

A MULTIFACETED BAYONET
This is a steel parade model of the most common bayonet that Civil War soldiers carried. Most were made of iron. The sides were not sharp, only the point. The men often used these bayonets as tent pegs. They also jammed them into tabletops or stumps and then used them as candlesticks. In a crisis, these bayonets also became handy digging tools.

Field artillery

CANNONS WERE the deadliest weapons in any Civil War fight. Most were made of bronze or steel and were loaded at the muzzle. Some were rifled. This means the insides of their barrels were cut with grooves that helped the cannonballs fly on long, straight paths. But the majority of the cannons were smoothbores. This means the insides of their barrels were smooth and had no grooves. This type of cannon could fire a wide variety of ammunition, but it was not as accurate as a rifled gun. To load one, a crew member wiped out the inside of the barrel with a wet sponge to put out any sparks from an earlier shot. Next a bag of gunpowder was stuffed into the barrel and pushed down to the bottom with a long pole called a rammer. Then a cannonball was placed in the barrel and pushed down. A crew member then jammed a long wire needle called a pick into a hole drilled into the barrel's base. The pick made a hole in the gunpowder bag. Next a fuse was placed into the hole at the barrel's base, and a long string was attached to a pin set into the top of the fuse. When the string was pulled, the pin popped out of the fuse, making a spark. The spark shot down into the barrel and hit the hole in the gunpowder bag made by the pick. At that point, the gunpowder exploded and sent the cannonball shooting out of the gun's mouth.

Telescope

TRAVELING THROUGH MUD
There were few paved roads in Civil War–era America. In rainy or snowy weather, thousands of marching soldiers and horses turned routes into muddy bogs. Artillerymen often had to dismount and help their huge draft horses pull heavy guns through the muck to reach the scene of the fighting. The soldiers were not always successful, and the unpassable roads sometimes saved armies from attack by opposing forces.

GUN LEVEL
This brass pendulum device is called a hausse. It was set at the base of the cannon barrel and told gunners if their weapon was level. It was necessary to level a gun to aim it.

Elevation gauge

Pendulum weight

Sight blade

GUN SIGHT
To aim a gun, a crewman set a portable sight on a weapon's base and lined it up with a simple blade sight that screwed into a spot on top of the muzzle. Some skilled cannoneers fashioned sights out of straight notched twigs.

Bubble level

Prolonge, a thick rope

Hitch

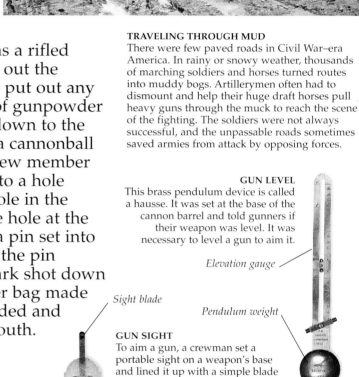

Carriage tail

MOVING GUNS ACROSS THE WATER
The hardest part of moving an army across a river was transporting its cannons. If there was time, the guns were disassembled and the pieces were floated across on small boats. When the army was in retreat or in pursuit of the enemy, fully assembled cannons were floated on pontoon boats or vessels made of waterproof blankets such as those shown here.

"NAPOLEON"
The most common cannon on the Civil War battlefield was the Model 1857 gun-howitzer. Soldiers called this smoothbore bronze gun a Napoleon. It was named after Louis-Napoléon, the emperor of France at the time. That ruler had sponsored the development of this gun and many other weapons.

CASE SHOT
The load shown here is a hollow iron shot filled with slugs and gunpowder. It is called case shot. A time fuse was screwed into the round opening in the ball. Case shot exploded in midair over the heads of attacking troops. Jagged fragments of the shell and its load of slugs rained down, killing or injuring the enemy.

Iron shot

Fuse hole

Solid iron ball

CANISTER ROUND
Smoothbore cannons could be used like large shotguns. As attacking troops raced toward an army's guns, artillerymen fired canister rounds at them. These were thin tin cans filled with heavy lead slugs and sawdust. They came apart at the cannon's mouth and sprayed deadly lead balls into enemy formations.

Lead slugs

GUNNER'S THUMB STALL
Before a cannon was reloaded, it was sponged out to kill any sparks inside. A gun crew member slipped this leather protective cover over his thumb and held it on top of the roasting-hot fuse hole at the cannon's base while the sponging continued. His thumb cut off the air supply to any burning debris in the gun.

Strapping

Sabot

Quarter-second marks

EXPLOSION TIMER
A simple pewter cap was screwed into case shot rounds. This one has three-, six-, and nine-second times stamped onto its face. It was invented by a Belgian army officer named Bormann and was called a Bormann fuse. Gunners punched a hole in the fuse face on the spot that indicated the number of seconds they wanted the fuse to burn.

SOLID SHOT AND SABOT
Solid iron cannonballs and hollow iron balls were strapped to a round piece of wood called a sabot. *Sabot* is the French word for "shoe." The wood piece kept the balls from rolling around in the ammunition chest and allowed them to sit well on top of a gunpowder bag inside a cannon barrel. The sabot and straps disintegrated when the cannon fired.

Cast-bronze tube

Leather vent cover to keep rainwater out of the tube

Detachable blade sight

Cascabel, used to maneuver the gun

Swab

Prolonge hook

Sponge

Rammer

Spoke

Hub

Iron wheel band

Wood wheel rim

Gettysburg

GETTYSBURG IS A SMALL TOWN in south-central Pennsylvania, just a few miles north of the Maryland state line. In the summer of 1863, Confederate General Robert E. Lee marched 75,000 men north to invade Union territory. They wandered into the Gettysburg area on July 1, looking for supplies. A small force of Union cavalry met and fought them there until thousands of Union army reinforcements arrived later. The commander of the federal forces, General George Meade, did not arrive until after dark. He led more than 88,000 troops. The next day, Meade's and Lee's men fought over important spots that bordered the town: a hill called Little Round Top, a grove of fruit trees called the Peach Orchard, farmland called the Wheat Field, and a rise near a burial ground called Cemetery Hill. These combats were so large that each was like a separate battle. On the morning of July 3, there was a fight around a spot called Culp's Hill. Then Lee ordered a division led by Major General George Pickett to attack the center of Meade's battle line. That afternoon attack is remembered as Pickett's Charge. Thousands of Confederates ran directly at Union cannons and rows of riflemen. A huge number of these Southerners were killed, wounded, or captured. This disaster forced Lee to accept defeat. He ordered his army to retreat south on July 4. His fight with Meade was the largest battle ever fought in North America.

MAJOR GENERAL MEADE
President Lincoln appointed George Meade commander of the Union's Army of the Potomac just two days before the Battle of Gettysburg. Meade was a native of Pennsylvania. He replaced General Joseph Hooker, who led the army when it was defeated in May, 1863, at the Battle of Chancellorsville, Virginia.

BATTLE VETERAN HARRY HAYS
Confederate General Harry Hays led troops in the desperate dusk attack on the Union army's position around the cemetery on July 2. He was defeated, but survived the battle. Later in the war, he was seriously wounded. He recovered and years later served as sheriff of New Orleans.

DUSK ATTACK
As the sun was setting on Thursday, July 2, two brigades from Confederate General Jubal Early's division rushed Union troops gathered around the gatehouse of Gettysburg's cemetery. They nearly succeeded in getting Meade's men off the hill. Then Union reinforcements pushed them back down, with many casualties. Newspaper artist Arthur Berghaus witnessed the fight and sketched this scene on the battlefield.

PICKETT'S CHARGE
Southerners in Pickett's Charge actually reached the Union battle lines. In this painting of the charge, Confederate General Lewis Armistead is seen in the background with his upraised sword beside a Union cannon. He was mortally wounded on the spot. Armistead was the highest-ranking Southerner to reach the Union line.

Gunner ramming in a canister round

Drum modeled on the instrument shown on the opposite page

Little Round Top

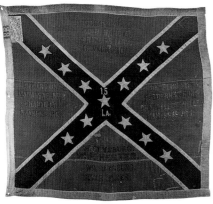

GETTYSBURG BATTLE HONORS

When a Union or Confederate regiment served honorably in a battle, it was permitted to stitch the name of that fight onto its battle flag. Here is the flag of the 15th Louisiana Regiment. Just below the center of its blue Saint Andrew's cross is stitched its Gettysburg battle honor. The men of the regiment carried this banner in that Pennsylvania fight.

GETTYSBURG DEAD

Photographers showed up at Gettysburg immediately after the battle. One used a stereo camera to take a picture of these dead Georgia and South Carolina soldiers. This photograph is one of a pair of pictures viewed with a stereopticon, a nineteenth-century 3-D viewer.

Main Union line in the valley below

LITTLE ROUND TOP

This hill gave soldiers a view of most of the Gettysburg battlefield. Both armies knew they needed to seize it if they wanted to win the fight. Georgia and Alabama troops charged it several times and were defeated by men of the 20th Maine Regiment. The Maine troops ran out of bullets, but they beat the Southerners by surprising them with a bayonet charge.

Animal hide drum head

A BATTLE DRUM

This drum was found on the battlefield. It was used as a model for a drum that is seen in a famous painting of the fight by artist Peter Rothermel. Drummers were often young boys who went into combat. They beat out signals on the drum that directed the troops to move one way or another.

Strapping to keep the drum head taut

Hand-painted eagle and crest

Small grove of trees that marked the center of Meade's lines

General Lewis Armistead

The siege of Vicksburg

CIVILIAN BOMB SHELTERS
Some Vicksburg citizens lived in what they called "dug outs" or "bomb proofs." As this photograph shows, these were simply holes dug into the town's hillsides. Some people dug these bomb proofs themselves. Others had their slaves do the digging. Sometimes poor whites also made dug outs, and then sold them to the town's upper classes.

Vicksburg, Mississippi, is a town on the east bank of the Mississippi River between Memphis, Tennessee, and New Orleans, Louisiana. The Confederate military greatly fortified Vicksburg and set up heavy cannons that could fire on any vessel passing the town. After the Union navy conquered New Orleans and Memphis in 1862, Vicksburg and Port Hudson, to its south, were the only points that kept the river closed to Union commerce and traffic. Vicksburg was also the last place where Confederate territory west of the Mississippi could pass troops and goods east to the rest of the South. Through late 1862 and half of 1863, Union commander Ulysses S. Grant sent several Northern forces there. Each campaign failed. Then in May, 1863, Grant maneuvered an army behind the town. After some small battles, he drove Vicksburg's defenders inside the town's trenches and fortifications. Meanwhile, the Union navy began shelling the garrison from the river. The town was surrounded by Grant's forces and besieged for more than forty days. No food or ammunition entered it. Both soldiers and civilians were reduced to eating mules and rats. Citizens lived in bomb shelters in hillsides. After more than a month of hunger, repeated attacks, and shelling by Northern forces, Confederate General John Pemberton surrendered the town on July 4.

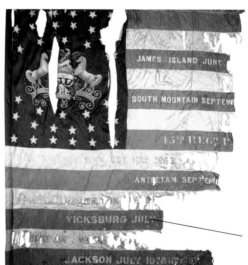

VICKSBURG HONORS
Regiments that served at Vicksburg were permitted to add the town's name to their list of battle honors. This meant the troops could stitch it onto their flag. Here the flag of the 51st Pennsylvania shows Vicksburg among the battle names sewn onto its tattered banner.

Battle honor

UNION TRENCHES AT VICKSBURG
The Mississippi sun is fierce in summer. Many Northern troops who were at Vicksburg came from cool-weather states such as Minnesota and Wisconsin. As this newspaper illustration shows, to ward off sunstroke and dehydration, these men put up canopies over their trenches. The trenches with "sun shades" surrounded Vicksburg on its eastern, land side.

THE COMMANDER AT VICKSBURG
Confederate General John C. Pemberton led the defense of Vicksburg. This photograph shows him in civilian dress. His defeat at Vicksburg cast a shadow over his Confederate military service. When angry Southerners were blaming him for the loss, many of them pointed out that John Pemberton was a native of Pennsylvania. He had married a Southern woman and thrown his loyalty behind her family and her part of the country when the war came.

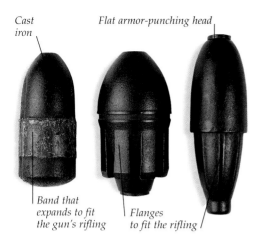

Cast
iron

Flat armor-punching head

Band that
expands to fit
the gun's rifling

Flanges
to fit the rifling

HEAVY ARTILLERY SHELLS
Union artillerymen brought heavy rifled cannons to Vicksburg. This assortment of shells for rifled artillery shows the grooves or fins that allowed these rounds to travel straight to their targets over long distances. Southern soldiers also used rifled guns. However, they were not able to replenish their supply of ammunition.

VICTORS MARCHING INTO TOWN
On Independence Day, July 4, 1863, Grant's troops marched into Vicksburg. This newspaper illustration shows the U.S. flag flying over the Vicksburg courthouse, the town's tallest landmark. This western Union victory followed by one day the Northern army's success at Gettysburg in Pennsylvania. Historians consider these back-to-back Union victories the beginning of the end for the Confederate war effort.

ATTACKING TRENCHES
The Vicksburg fight included infantry assaults. Early in the siege, Union foot soldiers rushed the Confederate trenches several times. Many of them were shot down as they tried to scale the sides of earthen ditches in front of Southern lines. Others were wounded or killed as they rushed across the open ground between their lines and Confederate trenches. After these assaults failed, Union cannons began firing on the town nonstop.

Stiff paper
to stabilize
fins

Steel
grenade
jacket

Lightweight
wood stem

Detonation plunger
plate exploded the
grenade.

A HAND GRENADE
Northerners tried several infantry assaults on the Vicksburg trench lines. In those attacks, they sometimes used Ketchum hand grenades. These weapons exploded when they landed on the detonation plates fixed to their noses. Confederates stopped these grenades by catching them in blankets and throwing them back at the attacking Union troops.

Northern life

CITIZENS OF NEW ENGLAND and the Midwest were stunned when the Southern states left the Union. Many had believed their family of states would never break up. When Confederates fired on Fort Sumter and the flag of the United States, that shock turned to anger. From Minneapolis to Philadelphia, people shouted for revenge. Men answered President Lincoln's call for army volunteers immediately. But unhappy Northerners had to wait for more than two years to hear about a satisfying military victory. Until July, 1863, Union armies were often losers on the battlefield. Through that period, the North's real success was on the homefront. Industries in Northern towns employed extra men and, in some places, allowed women into the workplace. Immigrants kept flowing into towns in Union states, and after President Lincoln signed the Homestead Act of 1862, many others headed west to make new homes on free frontier land. Theater performances, books, newspapers, and other forms of amusements were inexpensive and available to almost everyone. While Southerners were suffering shortages of food and clothing, and their rebellious nation was shrinking in size daily, the Union was growing larger and richer, and it never seemed to run out of new soldiers for its armies.

A TRAGIC FIRST LADY
Mary Todd Lincoln was from a Kentucky slave-holding family and had relatives who served in the Confederate military. When she married Abraham Lincoln in 1842, he was considered a bad catch. He came from a poor family and was self-educated. But Lincoln earned a modest fortune in the practice of law before being elected U.S. president in 1860. Sadly, two of their four sons died before Lincoln's assassination in 1865, and a third son died in 1871. Subsequently, Mrs. Lincoln suffered a series of emotional illnesses and was cared for by her eldest son, attorney Robert Lincoln. She died in 1882, while Robert was serving as a member of President James Garfield's cabinet.

A JOB FOR THE NEW CABINETMAKER.
From *Frank Leslie's Illustrated Newspaper*, February 2, 1861.

Wool tray

A WISHFUL CARTOON
Political cartoons were popular in Civil War–era magazines and illustrated newspapers. President Lincoln was often teased in them. But sometimes he was praised. This cartoon, published shortly after Lincoln's 1860 election victory, expressed the public's hope that the new leader could bring the nation back together.

A TOOL OF UNION VICTORY
Many historians claim Northern industry won the war for the Union. This steam-driven wool-carding machine from a Pennsylvania factory is an example of that. It made wool that could be turned into military uniforms. The South supplied manufacturers with cotton and other raw materials, but it lacked large amounts of machinery and free workers to make products for its own use. The loss of raw materials from the South did not cripple Northern industry. Union states simply purchased those items abroad. This allowed their factories to keep making uniforms, weapons, and equipment without interruption.

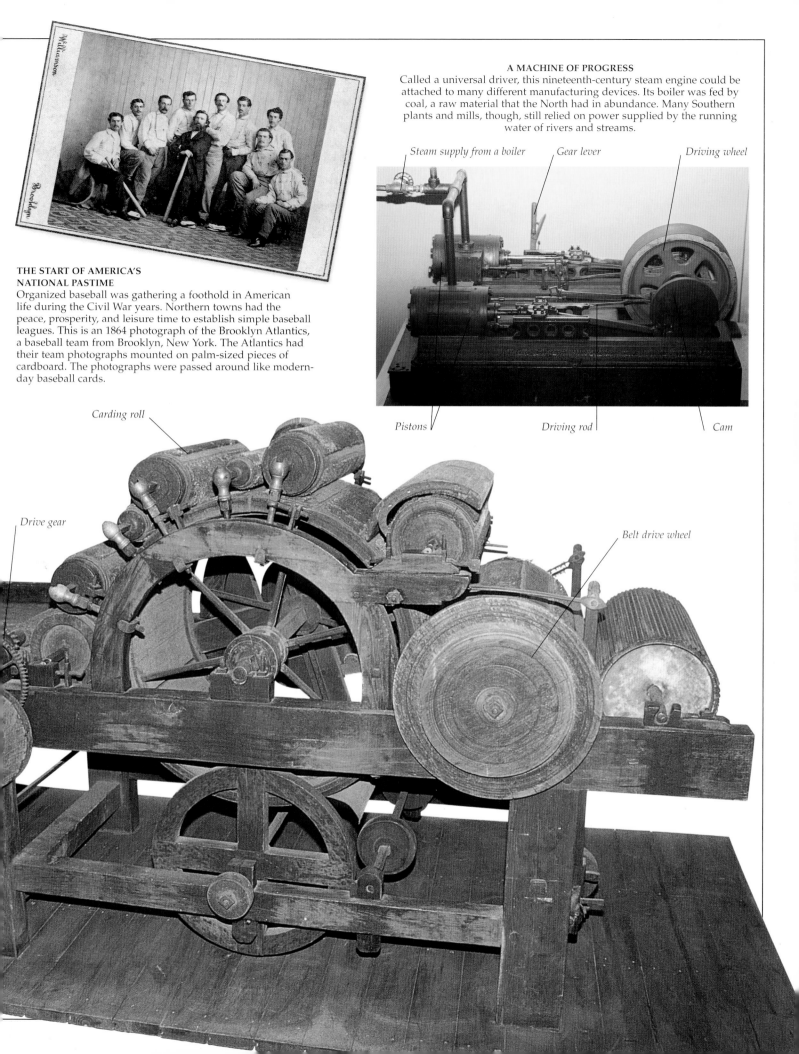

A MACHINE OF PROGRESS
Called a universal driver, this nineteenth-century steam engine could be attached to many different manufacturing devices. Its boiler was fed by coal, a raw material that the North had in abundance. Many Southern plants and mills, though, still relied on power supplied by the running water of rivers and streams.

Steam supply from a boiler

Gear lever

Driving wheel

Pistons

Driving rod

Cam

THE START OF AMERICA'S NATIONAL PASTIME
Organized baseball was gathering a foothold in American life during the Civil War years. Northern towns had the peace, prosperity, and leisure time to establish simple baseball leagues. This is an 1864 photograph of the Brooklyn Atlantics, a baseball team from Brooklyn, New York. The Atlantics had their team photographs mounted on palm-sized pieces of cardboard. The photographs were passed around like modern-day baseball cards.

Carding roll

Drive gear

Belt drive wheel

Confederate culture

THE CONFEDERATE STATES OF AMERICA existed for four years. It came into being when officials of the seceded states met to elect a leader in the spring of 1861. It died when Union troops occupied its capital city, Richmond, Virginia, in the spring of 1865. During those years, the people of this rebel nation tried to set up the institutions that citizens of more mature countries enjoyed. They chose a president and a vice president, elected members to a House of Representatives and a Senate, set up a Supreme Court, and appointed representatives to foreign governments. They also printed their own currency, raised a national flag, took the song "Dixie" as their national anthem, and adopted a constitution identical to the United States's document — except that the Confederate constitution contained an amendment guaranteeing the existence of slavery. The Confederacy also had national newspapers and magazines, supported theaters in its big towns, published patriotic poetry, and created its own legends and heroes.

THE SOUTHERN PRESS
The *Southern Illustrated News* was one of the few publications read throughout the South. It was modeled on Northern illustrated newspapers such as *Harper's Weekly*. Once Union forces interrupted Southern mail service, the newspaper's arrival in Confederate homes became irregular.

THE CONFEDERACY'S FIRST COUPLE
Jefferson Davis was the only president the Southern nation ever had. This is a copy of one of his official portraits. He was elected to a six-year term. Before taking that office, he was a U.S. senator, a member of President Franklin Pierce's cabinet, and a Mexican War hero. As a young man, he married the daughter of future U.S. President Zachary Taylor. His bride died just months after their wedding. Varina Howell Davis was the First Lady of the Confederate States of America. She was Davis's second wife and mother of their six children. She gave birth to one of those offspring in the Confederate White House in Richmond. Following her husband's death in 1889, she moved to New York City and supported herself as a professional writer.

Upright collar

Satin vest lapel

Cameo bracelet

Copy of an official portrait of Varina Davis

Fan

AT PLAY DURING THE WAR
Southerners tried to amuse themselves during the war years with games, books, and theater. These Confederate women are escaping their worries by playing a game of croquet on the lawn of their Virginia home, Patellus House.

WORTHLESS MONEY
At the start of the war, the Confederate government backed up its paper currency with gold kept in Southern and European banks. It also counted on backing up its money by exchanging cotton for gold in European markets. As the war went on, however, much of the South's gold was spent and it became hard to ship cotton abroad. Soon, food and clothing that had sold for $2 in the South cost $20. This was not because those things had really become much more expensive. It was because Confederate currency gradually became worth less and less as the conflict continued.

WARTIME SUBSTITUTES

This is the dress coat of Confederate General D. W. Adams. Regulations called for his uniform to be made of gray wool, but this coat is made of denim, the same cloth that is used to make blue jeans. In the war's last days, most Southerners wore and ate things made of substitute items because the Confederacy could not obtain good raw materials. Imitation coffee was made from the chicory plant. Flour was made from ground acorns. Quality items, such as real sugar, salt, and spices, were saved to be used as commodities for barter. In barter, people did not purchase necessities with money. They swapped valuable items for the things that they needed.

SOUTHERN INDUSTRY

Some historians have said the Confederacy was doomed because it lacked sophisticated industry. The Augusta, Georgia, gunpowder factory shown here illustrates that point. A material called niter was needed to manufacture explosives. This ingredient could not be obtained in quantity from Southern mines. Instead, factory chemists got niter by processing the contents of chamber pots they had collected throughout Augusta. Some locals later joked that they gave "their all" for the cause.

A SOUTHERN ARISTOCRAT

Caroline Deslonde was the daughter of an influential Creole plantation owner in Louisiana. Shortly before the Civil War began, she married Pierre Gustave Toutant Beauregard, one of the Confederacy's first hero-generals. Caroline was a member of what was known as the "Southern Aristocracy," the wealthy class of Southerners that had a strong influence on politics and society. Many working-class Confederates disliked these people and blamed them for the war and its hardships. After the conflict, the Southern Aristocracy was less prosperous, but it still remained influential in society and government.

President Jefferson Davis

Vice President Alexander Stephens

Mrs. Lucy Pickens, First Lady of South Carolina

Secretary of War George W. Randolph

General Thomas "Stonewall" Jackson

War on the water

THE NAVIES of the North and South played big parts in the strategies of Union and Confederate commanders. President Lincoln's sailors blocked Southern seaports and fought Confederates on the rivers. President Davis's navy commissioned privateers, vessels that attacked Union merchant ships all over the world and stole their cargoes. Both warring navies used America's lakes, bayous, and streams to transport soldiers to battlefields and forts, and fought to keep their opponents off the nation's waterways. The navies also changed the technology of warfare. The South produced the world's first modern ironclad warship. Built from the burned remains of the U.S. Navy vessel *Merrimac*, Confederates named it the CSS *Virginia*. Union inventor John Ericsson built an ironclad ship to fight it. His vessel was named the *Monitor*. Many other ironclads were made after that and fought battles along America's coasts and rivers. To defend against these and other vessels, Southern engineers perfected floating explosive mines. These devices threatened any ship entering Confederate waters.

ARMOR IN COMBAT
Iron armor was no guarantee of safety for navy fighting men. This newspaper illustration of the fight between the Union's iron-covered *Carondolet* and the South's armored *Arkansas* shows how the blast of one vessel's guns rocks the other. Shells fired at close range tore at the iron and splintered the metal plates' wood backing. Flying shards of metal and wood often killed or wounded the sailors inside.

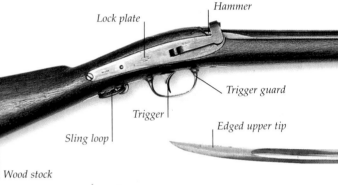

Hammer

Lock plate

Trigger guard

Trigger

Edged upper tip

Sling loop

Wood stock

A JENKS CARBINE
In Civil War navies, larger ships sometimes carried marines. These soldiers used rifles to defend the vessel. Sailors were often given short-barreled carbines because these weapons were easier to load in the cramped confines of a ship. This carbine is a potent .54 caliber Jenks breech loader. Both navies distributed this weapon in small numbers.

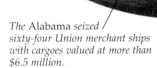

The Alabama *seized sixty-four Union merchant ships with cargoes valued at more than $6.5 million.*

THE *ALABAMA*
Commanded by Admiral Raphael Semmes, the Confederate raider *Alabama* was built secretly in Great Britain and had a crew of foreign volunteers. It attacked and sank Union merchant ships in the Atlantic and stalked the waters around Africa and the Mediterranean. The ship was sunk off Cherbourg, France, in a famous battle with the USS *Kearsarge*.

A SPYGLASS
The telescope was a basic tool of both navies. It allowed crews to observe enemy ships or survey a coastline from a safe distance. This Civil War spyglass is U.S. Navy issue.

A SEMISUBMERSIBLE
The Confederate vessel in this photograph is called a David. This class of vessel was semisubmersible. This means it took on some ballast and settled low in the water so that only its top was visible. It carried an explosive device attached to a wood beam. The beam jutted from the David's nose and was rammed into the side of an enemy ship. These vessels usually operated at night. Many attacked Union ships blockading South Carolina's Charleston Harbor.

Folding smokestack

Iron plates, held on with rivets *Armored paddle-wheel cover* *Sloping iron sides to deflect cannonballs*

Brass barrel band

Wood forestock

A UNION NAVY CUTLASS

Steel blade

Grip

Civil War sailors were expected to defend their ship from boarders. Though they carried carbines and revolvers, seamen in the 1860s still relied on "cold steel" in a fight. This Union navy cutlass was one of dozens of blades stored in a rack on a ship's main deck.

Brass hand guard

CSS *ARKANSAS*

This ten-gun Confederate vessel served on the Mississippi and Yazoo Rivers, fighting around Vicksburg. It was armored with railroad rails and iron plates, and was pushed along by two propellers. As a Union fleet approached the ironclad near Baton Rouge, Louisiana, in August, 1862, its engines broke down. To keep it out of Union hands, the crew set it on fire and abandoned it. The *Arkansas* floated downriver and sank.

MINES IN POSITION

This newspaper illustration shows how wood mines were floated just below the surface of the water. America's use of mines during its civil war caused international debate. Many nations believed that the use of submerged explosives was cowardly, as well as a violation of the rules of warfare.

A UNION MINE SWEEPER

This is the Union ironclad *Saugus* on Virginia's James River. It is fitted with a crude net that juts from its prow. A brave Union naval officer stands on a platform above the net. He directs the ironclad left or right to net or sweep up an explosive mine. If the device explodes, the officer could be injured or killed.

A NINETEENTH-CENTURY MINE

Wood or tin containers of explosives were positioned in harbors and rivers. Called torpedoes or mines, some of them were fitted with detonators. If a passing ship struck one of the mines, it exploded and sank the vessel. Other mines had insulated electrical wires that ran to a spot on the shore. An operator hiding there could touch the wire to a crude battery and explode the mine, sinking a ship. The mine shown here is made of wood with iron strapping.

The secret war

LONG BEFORE THE CIVIL WAR, soldiers knew to watch out for civilians who banded together to attack the troops and destroy the property of conquering armies. These combatants were called guerrillas and saboteurs. Virginia attorney John Mosby organized a group of such men to operate in Virginia's Blue Ridge Mountain region. They called themselves Partisan Rangers, and at night they often rode behind enemy lines to attack and capture Union troops. During the day, they disappeared into mountain hideouts or Confederate homes and were difficult to catch. Spies were another danger, reporting military plans and movements to the enemy. This secret warfare is called espionage. It was easy to carry out in the United States, because the opponents looked alike, shared the same culture, and spoke the same language. Elizabeth Van Lew of Richmond, Virginia, was very successful at it. She was a mature single woman who held strong pro-Union opinions, but was a member of a wealthy, well-known family living in the Confederate capital. Van Lew pretended to suffer from mild mental illness and acted in eccentric ways. As a consequence, when Southern government leaders gathered in her family's home or around the town, they spoke freely in her presence, believing she was harmless. Using couriers, Van Lew sent word of what she heard to Union military commanders. When the war ended, she received the thanks of General Ulysses S. Grant, the general in chief of the Union army.

A HANGED SPY
Spies caught disguised in their enemy's military uniforms were quickly disposed of. Lawrence Orton Williams was a cousin of Mrs. Robert E. Lee. Union troops caught him wearing a U.S. Army uniform. Williams claimed to be a member of the inspector general's staff. He was questioned, then hanged.

A SUCCESSFUL SPY
This may be the only photograph of William Henry Harrison, a Confederate army officer who worked as a scout and spy. He won his place in history by pinpointing Union army positions during General Robert E. Lee's invasion of the North in summer, 1863, bringing on the Battle of Gettysburg. Here he holds a coded message that reads "I Love You."

THE GRAY GHOST
John Mosby was a slender man. Arming himself with up to eight revolvers, he rode out at night in a plumed hat and cape to gather his guerrilla band. The men would attack Union troops, supply depots, and camps. In the South, he was a hero — always beating an opponent, always escaping capture. To Union troops, he was the "Gray Ghost," a danger of the night. Years later, Mosby became a folk hero to veterans on both sides of the conflict.

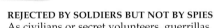
Center-fire hammer *Front blade sight* *Load ejector* *Recessed trigger* *Walnut grip*

REJECTED BY SOLDIERS BUT NOT BY SPIES
As civilians or secret volunteers, guerrillas, spies, and saboteurs used any weapon that came to hand to carry on their underground war. Many of their arms were military rejects. The Allen & Wheelock center-fire pistol shown here was manufactured as a .44 caliber "Army" revolver, but never widely used by the military. However, firearms like it were popular in covert operations.

BOTH A DETECTIVE AND SPY
At the start of the Civil War, Allen Pinkerton was a successful private detective. Union General George McClellan hired him to organize a corps of spies for his army. But Pinkerton was not good at espionage. He often overestimated the size of the Southern forces. It is surprising that Pinkerton allowed himself to be photographed. Good spies rarely want anyone to know what they look like.

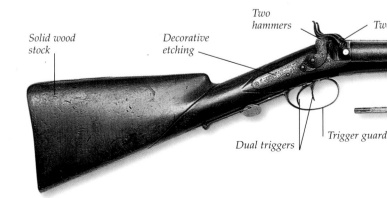
Solid wood stock *Decorative etching* *Two hammers* *Two nipples* *Dual triggers* *Trigger guard*

MOSBY'S PARTISAN RANGERS ATTACK

Mosby was well known to Northerners. Union tabloids carried stories about the man Yankee soldiers called the Gray Ghost. He and his troops were famous for attacking Union soldiers and then slipping away without a trace. This newspaper illustration shows an assault by Mosby's men on a Union army wagon train near the Blue Ridge Mountains in Virginia.

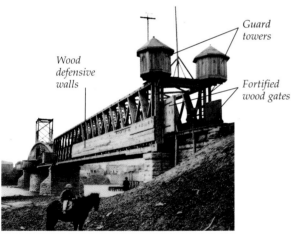

Wood defensive walls

Guard towers

Fortified wood gates

THE SOCIALITE SPY

Young Washington, D.C., widow Rose O'Neill Greenhow was a socialite known and liked by Union government leaders. She threw parties where war business was discussed, and supposedly charmed men into telling her some military secrets. She was also a Confederate spy. Eventually, she was caught by Union police and imprisoned in Washington's Old Capitol Prison. This photograph of Mrs. Greenhow and her daughter was taken there.

PROTECTING A BRIDGE

Saboteurs, people who destroy enemy facilities and equipment, found wood military bridges easy targets. They could be soaked with kerosene and burned down. Union troops sometimes protected them from saboteurs and guerrilla attacks by fortifying them with walls, and putting gates and guard towers at both ends. These structures turned the bridge into a wooden fort.

Double-barrel design

Metal loop to hold ramrod

Wood ramrod

A GUERRILLA FAVORITE

Shotguns were popular weapons with guerrillas and troops like Mosby's Partisan Rangers. They were often sawed off and used in running fights with Union cavalry troopers. A shotgun packed as much punch as a pistol and could hit more than one soldier at a time. The weapon shown here is a 12-gauge muzzle loader carried by a Confederate.

The March to the Sea

UNION MAJOR GENERAL William T. Sherman's campaign to capture Atlanta was the first step in his plan to crush Georgia. His army marched south from Chattanooga, Tennessee, in the summer of 1864, fighting battle after battle with the Confederates' Army of Tennessee. Sherman penned Southern forces in Atlanta, then forced them to abandon it. His troops rested there from September 2 to November 12, then burned much of the city to the ground. From November 15 to December 20, Sherman's men marched west to the city of Savannah on Georgia's Atlantic coast. All along their route, the soldiers burned homes and towns. They took the food of civilian families and destroyed any food and crops they could not use. The civilians they left behind were usually homeless and hungry. Sherman said he wanted "to make all Georgia howl." He did. The Confederate army was unable to gather enough troops in front of Sherman's soldiers to stop them. When the Union army arrived in front of Savannah, the Confederates' Fort McAllister could not resist it and surrendered after a fifteen-minute fight. On December 21, Savannah's Confederate commander, General William J. Hardee, had his troops leave the city. Union troops paraded through the streets, celebrating their victory.

General Oliver O. Howard
General William T. Sherman
General John Logan
General Henry Slocum

SHERMAN AND HIS OFFICERS
The men around General Sherman are the generals who led his men to Savannah. General Logan, a Democratic congressman before the war, returned to politics when peace came. He helped establish the holiday now known as Memorial Day. Originally it honored only Civil War dead. Today it honors all U.S. military personnel who died defending their country.

THE CITY OF ATLANTA IS CONQUERED
This home was built on the outskirts of Atlanta. Unfortunately for its owner, it sat right along the Confederate army's main defense line and was riddled by Union cannon fire.

ATLANTA'S RAILROADS DESTROYED
Confederate General John Bell Hood commanded the troops inside Atlanta. As he retreated from the city, he had his men destroy Atlanta's railroad roundhouse and burn railroad cars filled with ammunition. The explosions could be heard for miles. This photograph shows all that remained.

"QUAKER" GUNS

Sherman's men ran into small Confederate fortifications along the March to the Sea. But many of them were deserted or had just a few soldiers inside. Sometimes these forts' "cannons" were really logs that had been cut and painted to look as though they were big guns when seen from a distance. Soldiers called them "Quaker" guns, after the pacifist Christian sect known as Quakers. This painting done by a Union veteran shows soldiers surprised at discovering that they were only threatened by logs.

AN AGING DRAFTEE

This is a photograph of Danish immigrant Charles Stevens and his little girl Mary Henrietta. Stevens came to the United States before the Civil War and settled in Savannah. At the age of forty-eight, he was considered too old to serve in the Confederate army; but as Sherman's army approached, Stevens was pressed into a local militia unit. He was captured by Union soldiers and later died of disease in a prisoner-of-war camp.

A DEMOLISHED GEORGIA HOME

This picture of Union soldiers resting among the rubble of a Georgia house was taken outside Atlanta. The destruction is remarkable. Even the home's window frames are removed. There are no known photographs of similar destruction along the March to the Sea. The Northern army moved too rapidly and was too spread out to be captured easily with slow, old-fashioned nineteenth-century photographic equipment.

SAVANNAH'S COMMANDER

Confederate General William J. Hardee commanded the soldiers inside the city of Savannah. Although his few troops could not possibly have won against Sherman's large force, his defeat marred his military reputation. William Hardee was an intelligent professional soldier. Before the Civil War, he had written the training manual used by all recruits in both the Northern and Southern armies.

A VICTORY PARADE THROUGH SAVANNAH

This is a newspaper artist's rough sketch of the victory parade of Sherman's army through downtown Savannah. Union soldiers spared this attractive old city. Some places shown here still stand.

The Confederacy surrenders

GRANT'S ARMY BESIEGED Lee's forces at Petersburg, Virginia, from June, 1864, until April, 1865. At the same time, Sherman's Union troops took the cities of Atlanta, Savannah, and Charleston, as well as Columbia, South Carolina, and Raleigh, North Carolina. In December, 1864, Confederate General John Bell Hood tried to overcome Union forces at Nashville, Tennessee. His army was crushed. Then, on April 1, 1865, Union troops overran Confederates near Petersburg in a battle called Five Forks. This led to the collapse of Lee's defenses. Confederate government officials abandoned nearby Richmond, and Lee's army retreated toward Appomattox Court House, Virginia. Grant's forces surrounded Lee's there, and on April 9, Lee surrendered. Soon afterward, Confederate generals Joseph Johnston and Kirby Smith also surrendered their armies. On June 23, General Stand Watie, commander of Confederate Native American troops, had his soldiers lay down their arms at Doaksville in Indian Territory. This put an informal end to America's deadliest war.

MEETING IN PEACE
Officers of Sherman's and Johnston's armies mingle around the North Carolina home of James Bennett, the site of their generals' surrender negotiations. These talks continued for a few days, because Union authorities did not approve of Sherman's first offer to the surrendering Confederates. They believed the terms were too lenient.

Officers standing out of rifle range

IN THE TRENCHES AT WAR'S END
The last months of the war around Petersburg, Virginia, saw Union and Confederate soldiers fighting from trenches. These Union troops are resting behind the trench lines before moving forward to resume fighting. Hundreds of soldiers died around Petersburg from artillery fire, snipers, and mass attacks on each army's flanks.

Jubilant slaves   *U.S.C.T. regiment*   *Scavengers*

UNION TROOPS IN THE CONFEDERATE CAPITAL
When President Jefferson Davis, his cabinet, and other government officials fled Richmond, the city's people panicked. Jails and hospitals were broken open, criminals and army deserters began looting, and fires broke out. The capital was already a burning wreck when the black Union troops shown in this newspaper illustration walked into the city. They met with no resistance.

WHERE THE WAR ENDED
Four years of bloody civil war came to an end in the tiny parlor of Wilmer McClean's house. It was there that Lee signed a surrender document prepared by Grant. Today the McClean house is a National Historic Landmark.

LEE IN DEFEAT
After his meeting with Grant, Robert E. Lee packed his personal belongings and rode away alone to find his family. A few days later, he put on his Confederate uniform one last time and posed on the back porch of the house his wife had rented in Richmond. Famous Civil War photographer Mathew Brady, a Northerner, took this photograph.

THE SOUTH IN RUINS
The war ended with entire Southern cities destroyed by fire. Many thousands of people were homeless. Former slaves wandered the countryside looking for refugee relief. Defeated soldiers clogged roads on their long walks home. The places where these wandering people rested often looked like this photograph of Columbia, the destroyed capital of South Carolina. There was little shelter and no food to be had.

Union Lieutenant Colonel Eli Parker, Grant's military secretary

Union General Ulysses S. Grant

Confederate General Robert E. Lee

Union Major General Philip Sheridan

TWO MILITARY LEADERS MEET
Surrounded by Union troops near the village of Appomattox Court House, General Robert E. Lee sent a note to General Ulysses S. Grant. In it, he asked for surrender terms. Grant met Lee in a nearby house just outside the hamlet, and there accepted the surrender of the Confederate army. Lee's troops were allowed to find their own way home. In addition, his officers could keep their mounts and sidearms. Some of the Southern veterans walked hundreds of miles to reach their homes and families again.

The fates of two leaders

WITHIN DAYS OF LEE'S SURRENDER, the Union lost its leader. On the evening of April 14, 1865, President Abraham Lincoln, First Lady Mary Todd Lincoln, and their friends Clara Harris and Major Henry Rathbone went to Ford's Theatre in Washington, D.C., to see the play *Our American Cousin.* An actor named John Wilkes Booth slipped behind the president's seat and shot him in the back of the head. When Rathbone went after Booth, the assassin slashed him with a knife. Then he leaped to the stage, shouted,*"Sic semper tyrannus"* ("So always to tyrants"), and escaped on horseback. Federal troops and local police officers immediately began a manhunt. Lincoln died of his wound the next morning. Vice President Andrew Johnson assumed the office of chief executive. On April 24, Union cavalry trapped Booth in a barn on a Virginia farm and killed him. Meanwhile, several of Booth's associates were arrested for helping him in the assassination plot. They were convicted of their crimes on June 30. Four were hanged. The rest were given long prison terms. While these events were unfolding, U.S. troops were also searching for Confederate President Jefferson Davis. He and his cabinet members had disappeared from Richmond on April 2. Although federal officials were not sure what to do with Davis, they did not want him to escape the country. Weeks later, Davis and his escort were captured near Irwinville, Georgia. By May 22, Davis was imprisoned at Fort Monroe, Virginia, and remained there for two years. He spent his last years writing his memoirs.

THE SCENE OF THE CRIME
Ford's Theatre, where Abraham Lincoln was murdered, was owned by John Ford. He and many actors, as well as others who knew John Wilkes Booth, were detained by federal authorities after the assassination of the president. The theater was closed. However, today it is a National Historic Landmark. Tours of it are given, and occasionally it is used for special theatrical productions.

THE CONFEDERACY'S PRESIDENT IN CUSTODY
Jefferson Davis's wife and family were with him when he was captured by Union soldiers. They and other members of their party were placed in canvas-covered ambulances and driven into Macon, Georgia. This is the only known photograph of the group in custody. The ambulances are surrounded by cavalrymen. Mrs. Davis and the children were later forcibly separated from the former Confederate president. They did not see or hear from him until many months later.

DAVIS'S LAST FLAG
This Confederate battle flag was carried by Jefferson Davis's personal military escort during the former president's flight from U.S. troops. Davis, determined to avoid capture, was armed with a powerful Henry repeating rifle. He and his party were seized in Georgia one night while they were gathered around a campfire. Not a shot was fired.

THE MURDER OF A PRESIDENT
This old lithograph illustrates the events of April 14, 1865. After the shooting, the unconscious president was carried across the street from the theater to the small home owned by a tailor named Petersen. Lincoln passed away there near dawn the next day.

Knife used to slash Major Rathbone

Booth's single-shot derringer

Mary Todd Lincoln

Clara Harris

Major Henry Rathbone

PLAYING AT FORD'S THEATRE
This is a playbill for the feature performed at Ford's Theatre the night of April 14. Laura Keene, the star of *Our American Cousin,* knew Booth. She was briefly detained by the police. However, she had no part in the plot to kill the president.

DAVIS'S DUNGEON PRISON
Jefferson Davis was held in a dank dungeon cell inside the stone walls of Fort Monroe, Virginia. He was never out of sight of the guards, and for a long time he was manacled to an iron ball and chain. A jury was selected in anticipation of a trial in which he would be charged with various crimes against the United States. However, no trial was ever held. After two years of confinement, Davis was bailed out of prison with funds raised by Northern newspaper publisher Horace Greeley.

ONE OF THE CONSPIRATORS
Mary Surratt ran a Washington, D.C., boardinghouse. Booth and several conspirators involved in his plot to kill the president and other government officials often met there. She was convicted of taking part in the plot, and was the first woman ever executed by the federal government. Surratt and three men who were convicted of the same crime were hanged on July 7, 1865.

ANOTHER MEMBER OF THE PLOT
This is a police mug shot of Lewis Powell, alias Lewis Paine. A very tall and strong young man, Powell was a former member of John Mosby's Confederate guerrilla outfit, the Partisan Rangers. As Booth was shooting Lincoln, Powell was attacking Secretary of State William Seward. That murder attempt was not successful. Others in the plot were to kill Vice President Johnson and General Grant. They also failed. Powell was arrested, charged with helping Booth, convicted, and hanged.

Handcuffs

A life of freedom

CHEERS FOR THEIR LIBERATOR
On April 5, 1865, President Abraham Lincoln toured the newly conquered Confederate capital of Richmond, Virginia. As he rode around the town, he was cheered everywhere by newly freed black men and women. Although the president had issued his final Emancipation Proclamation two years previously, the ex-slaves had only recently learned of it.

AFTER MORE THAN two hundred years of bondage, America's slaves were freed when the Thirteenth Amendment to the U.S. Constitution was passed in December, 1865. However, by then slavery was already dead. More than six months had passed since the last fight of the Civil War. Across the South, black Americans wandered the countryside looking for a new start in life. To deal with these estimated 4 million people, the federal government established the Freedmen's Bureau. This agency set up villages to house and feed refugees, and schools to educate them. Meanwhile, opportunistic Northerners, called Carpetbaggers because they usually carried their few possessions in suitcases made of carpet material, tried to gain the political support of freedmen. Former slaves had been given voting rights under recently passed laws. To win their votes, some Carpetbagger politicians said black voters might get forty acres of land and a mule to start their own farms. This cruel lie created false hope among displaced Southern blacks. Many of them returned to their former masters' plantations and worked there again as poorly paid employees. Some headed for the Western territories or Northern cities. Others helped rebuild the South to make it a good home for themselves and their families.

FREE AT LAST
Most slaves in the Deep South did not know of Abraham Lincoln's Emancipation Proclamation until Union occupation forces came to their communities and read the document to them. This old artwork showing a black Union trooper reading the proclamation to newly freed men and women recalls that experience. The news that freedom had finally come after centuries of pleading and prayer stunned most blacks who heard it. Many were overcome with joy and immediately set out for other parts of the United States, where they hoped to begin new lives.

Military-style tunic

A SYMBOL OF FREEDOM
This unidentified freedman had his photograph taken in a commercial photographic studio in Louisiana. That a Southern black man could walk into a white photographer's place of business, pose, and pay for his picture like a white patron did was a civil rights victory. This photograph is quiet yet significant evidence that life in the postwar South was changing.

Lynching victim

TERRORS OF THE NIGHT
After the war, there were many groups of hooded night riders that terrorized ex-slaves, federal officials, Carpetbaggers, and sympathetic Southerners. The lynchings and beatings that they carried out were documented in the Northern press with drawings such as this one. Some groups, such as the Knights of the White Camelia, broke up after their targets had understood that the messages these terrorists conveyed were to be obeyed. The Ku Klux Klan, however, rebuffed calls from many ex-Confederates to disband and set itself up as a powerful and violent underground government in the postwar South.

A HOME FOR FREEDMEN
This settlement for homeless ex-slaves looks like a series of army barracks. Other settlements looked like a collection of cottages. Many of these first refugee "villages" were built either by soldiers or by government laborers. Later, the Freedmen's Bureau hired refugees to do some of the building themselves.

FREED AND UNEMPLOYED
These South Carolina slaves have been freed by Northern army troops. But their former master's land, the Drayton Plantation, is producing nothing and they are without a means of supporting themselves. This was a common hazard that came with freedom. Some plantation owners ran away from advancing Union armies and left their slaves without food or clothing. But in the months after the war, some former slaves and slave owners reunited, working together as employers and employees.

THREATENING A FREE FAMILY
When freedmen were given the right to vote, some former Confederates organized themselves into terrorist bands to intimidate them. The Ku Klux Klan was the most famous of these groups. Early in Reconstruction, its members would burst into the homes of black people and tell the men: Do not vote for any Carpetbaggers.

A new era begins

FOR MORE THAN TEN YEARS after the Civil War, the South was occupied by federal troops. This period in U.S. history is known as Reconstruction. Former Confederate government officials were prohibited from holding public offices. Confederate veterans were required to take an oath of allegiance to the United States in order to enjoy some of the benefits of citizenship. Some ex-Confederates never regained the right to vote. Meanwhile, newly freed slaves were encouraged to vote in local elections. Several African Americans were appointed to positions in federal and local government, and some became members of the U.S. House of Representatives. Ambitious Carpetbaggers moved into towns throughout the South. They started or bought out businesses and took over local government positions. Southerners who cooperated with the Carpetbaggers were called Scalawags. Angry Southerners formed secret terrorist groups that rode out at night and murdered, whipped, or intimidated Carpetbaggers, Scalawags, and newly freed blacks. Federal troops provided what little law and order there was in those communities. Elsewhere, though, the future looked bright. Elected president in 1868, Ulysses S. Grant served two terms and presided over the industrial expansion of the rest of the nation and the settlement of the Western frontier. And in 1876, the United States celebrated its centennial. Many of the festivities were held in Philadelphia, Pennsylvania, the nation's birthplace. At an industrial exhibition that was staged there, some of the public displays featured technological wonders. Others praised the nation's people for reuniting and again living in peace.

A POPULAR PRESIDENT
Ulysses S. Grant enjoyed the voting support of most Union army veterans. Despite several financial scandals within his administration, Grant was always popular with the public. His vision of America's future was farsighted. While touring the South in the 1870s, he spoke to black church members in Memphis, Tennessee. He thanked them for their support and talked of their place in politics. No other president would make similar gestures for many more years.

A VETERAN'S ORPHANS
No story explained the healing between North and South better than the tale of General John Bell Hood's children. Hood went off to war a handsome young bachelor. By the time it ended, he was a general in a defeated army. He was also crippled. He had lost a leg and the use of one arm from wounds suffered in two separate battles. Despite his disabilities, Hood married and fathered many children, most of them twins. He also pursued a business career in New Orleans, where he was admired for his ambitious postwar outlook. In the 1870s, he, his wife, and their oldest child died in a yellow fever epidemic. Confederate veterans looked to his surviving children's care and circulated this photograph of them, searching for adoptive parents. All of the Hood orphans were eventually adopted, by families from the North as well as the South.

John C. Breckinridge

SOUTHERNERS IN EXILE
This group of ex-Confederates fled to Canada after the Civil War. When their government collapsed, they feared punishment by Union authorities, as had happened in other countries when revolutions failed. One of these men, John C. Breckinridge, was an 1860 candidate for U.S. president and a former Confederate general. Neither he nor the other men with him were punished for having taken part in the conflict. Breckinridge later returned to the United States and became governor of Kentucky.

A UNITED NATION
This painting commemorates the joining of the Union Pacific and Central Pacific railroads, from east and west, at Promontory Point, Utah, in 1869. There railroad officials completed the first transcontinental railroad by connecting the last rails with a gold spike — and literally pulling all parts of the United States together.

A SOLDIER'S FUNERAL
Robert E. Lee died in 1870 at the age of sixty-three. This is a photograph of his funeral ceremony. At the time of his death, Lee was president of Washington College in Lynchburg, Virginia. Today the school is known as Washington & Lee University. In his later years, Lee was lauded in the North because he encouraged Southerners to embrace peace, a place for free blacks in American society, and America's future.

Washington College's chapel

THE GREAT CENTENNIAL
Independence Day, 1876, marked America's one hundredth birthday, its centennial. On the west coast, there were patriotic demonstrations and a great naval display in San Francisco Bay. On the east coast, there was a great fair in Philadelphia, where all the marvels of technology were displayed. One of those was this great Corliss engine. Machines like it promised work and prosperity for the reunited American people.

Saxhorn   *Bass drum*   *Louisiana state flag*   *U.S. flag*

CARPETBAG POLITICS
This is a relic from American politics. It is a bandwagon. In the postwar years, a candidate would have a band travel around a community in a wagon, playing for the public and gathering support for him. This Carpetbagger candidate's bandwagon was used during a campaign for the federally controlled Louisiana legislature. During Reconstruction in the South, no candidate could run for election without the approval of federal officials.

Index

Acknowledgements

The author and Dorling Kindersley Publishing offer their grateful thanks for assistance in creating this book to: the Confederate Memorial Hall, New Orleans, LA; the Gettysburg National Military Park, Gettysburg, PA; the Old Capitol Museum of Mississippi, Jackson, MS; the U.S. Army Military History Institute, Carlisle, PA; the William Penn Museum, Pennsylvania State Museum Commission, Harrisburg, PA; the Louisiana State Museum, New Orleans, LA; the National Civil War Museum, Harrisburg, PA; Herb Peck, Jr.; Joe Baughman; Lloyd Ostendorf; the Cincinnati Museum of Art, Cincinnati, OH; the Massachusetts Historical Society, Boston, MA; the Chicago Historical Society, Chicago, IL; and Corbis Images, New York, NY. Endpapers map and image colorization provided by Slimfilms, New York, NY.

Photography Credits:
t = top; b = bottom; l = left; r = right; c = center
Collection of Joseph Baughman 35t. *Century Magazine* 26bl, 26tr, 46l, 63tr. **Chicago Historical Society** 6tc, 9t. *Civil War Times Illustrated* **Collection Prints** 6tl, 6bl, 15tl, 15b, 17lc, 18bl, 21tr, 21trc, 23br, 27t, 30bc, 33tr, 35bl, 35br, 36tl, 36c, 39bl, 40tr, 41tl, 43cl, 43tr. **Confederate Memorial Hall, New Orleans, LA** 14t, 14lc, 15r, 16rc, 17lc, 23rc, 24tl, 24lc, 24lbc, 27lc, 27rc, 28tl, 28bl, 29rc, 30rc, 31tr, 32tl, 32lc, 33br, 34br, 36blc, 37tl, 37tr, 37c, 37bl, 38br, 38bl, 38c, 39tr, 39trc, 40tl, 40rc, 40lc, 41tc, 42bl, 43tl, 49tl, 49rc, 49b, 50lc, 50br, 51rc, 52rc, 52-53rc, 61rc, 62lc, 62bl. **Barnaby Conrad Collection, Carpenteria, CA** 52bl. **Corbis** 6bc, 12tr, 13bl, 13br, 13tr, 18br, 19lc, 20c, 21br, 23bl, 25l, 30lc, 31lc, 31bc, 35lc, 38-39tc, 40bl, 47tl, 52bl, 54tc, 54bc, 56tr, 57t, 57br, 58cr, 59tr, 59br, 60b, 61tl, 61bl,

62tl, 63tl. **William C. Davis Collection** 62br. *Frank Leslie's Illustrated Newspaper* 14b, 16b, 17b, 26-27bc, 34c, 42lc, 44bl, 45tr, 50-51tc, 51lcb, 53t, 56lc, 56lb, 60tl. **Gettysburg National Military Park** 16-17tc, 24brc, 24b, 29t, 32cb, 32b, 33tr, 33trc, 33rc, 36tr, 36b, 37br, 39bl, 39br, 40-41bc, 41tl, 41tlc, 41tc, 41tr, 45tl, 45br, 50ct, 50cb. **Jack G. Grothe Collection** 19bl. **John O. Hess** 22br. **Illinois State Historical Association** 32tr. **International Museum of Photography, Rochester, NY** 33br. **Kansas State Historical Society** 7br. **Library of Congress** 7t, 7bl, 11bl, 19tr, 22br, 26c, 29bc, 33bl, 46tr, 48c, 49cl, 49tr, 50tr, 51br, 54bl, 55br, 58tr, 61bl. **Lincoln Museum, Harrowgate, TN** 34l. **Louisiana Historical Association** 25r. **Louisiana State Museum** 8tr, 8bl. **Department of Archives & Manuscripts, Louisiana State University** 63b. **Commonwealth of Massachusetts** 19tcr. **Massachusetts Historical Society** 12tl. **Collection of Michael J. McAfee** 18-19tc. **State Archives of Michigan** 21c. **National**

Archives 10tr, 11br, 14tr, 19br, 50bc, 53br, 58-59c, 59bc, 59br. **The National Civil War Museum** 10r. **National Park Service** 57b. **National Portrait Gallery** 33tr, 33bl, 42tr. **Old Capitol Museum of Mississippi History** 16cl, 36lc, 48bl. **Old Court House Museum, Vicksburg, MS** 44t. **Ruth Koerner Oliver Collection** 45bl. **Lloyd Ostendorf Collection** 10br, 20bl. **Charles E. Pearson Collection** 55tr. **Pennsylvania State Museum** 42-43bc, 43cr, 44rc, 46-47bc, 47tr. **Fanny U. Phillips** 20rc. **Marian B. Ralph Collection** 52lc. **Smithsonian Institution** 11t. **Union League Club** 22tl. **U.S. Army Military History Institute** 8c, 8-9c, 12bl, 12br, 21tl, 24tcr, 26c, 28br, 29lc, 29br, 53lc, 55lc, 58bl, 61c. **U.S. Naval History Institute** 27br. **U.S. Navy** 51bl. **Valentine Museum, Richmond, VA** 19trc, 30tl. **Vermont Historical Association** 34tl. **Library of Virginia** 48tl. **Washington & Lee University** 63c. **Kean Wilcox Collection** 23tl. **Collection of Shelby Young, Memphis, TN** 9tr.

DAKOTA TERRITORY

Civil War America

THESE COLORED AREAS show the lands that made up the United States and the Confederate States of America at the time of the Civil War. More than ten thousand combats took place between 1861 and 1865. Only a few of the largest or most important ones are shown. Virginia and Tennessee saw most of the military action. The 100 miles between Washington, D.C., and Richmond, Virginia, were fought over so often and were so badly shell-torn that they were almost unlivable by the end of the conflict.

MINNESOTA

WISCONSIN

LAKE

IOWA

ILLINOIS

COLORADO TERRITORY

KANSAS

MISSOURI

WILSON'S CREEK

PEA RIDGE

PUBLIC LAND

INDIAN TERRITORY

DOAKSVILLE

ARKANSAS

NEW MEXICO TERRITORY

MISSISSIPPI RIVER

VICKSBURG

LOUISIANA

PORT HUDSON

TEXAS

BATON ROUGE

MEXICO